ACHIEVING COHERENCE IN DISTRICT IMPROVEMENT

ACHIEVING COHERENCE IN DISTRICT IMPROVEMENT

Managing the Relationship Between the Central Office and Schools

Susan Moore Johnson
Geoff Marietta
Monica C. Higgins
Karen L. Mapp
Allen Grossman

Harvard Education Press
Cambridge, Massachusetts

Library of Congress Control Number 2014959083

Paperback ISBN 978-1-61250-811-5
Library Edition ISBN 978-1-61250-812-2

Published by Harvard Education Press,
an imprint of the Harvard Education Publishing Group

Harvard Education Press
8 Story Street
Cambridge, MA 02138

Cover Design: Ciano Design
Cover Photo: © Image Source/Corbis
The typefaces used in this book are Minion and DIN.

CONTENTS

Introduction

As Jackie Morris opened her laptop to begin work on July 1, she silently celebrated the beginning of her second year as superintendent of Bowen County Public Schools (BCPS). Over the past twelve months, she had earned the respect of principals and teachers, gained support in the community, and won the endorsement of her school board. However, she realized that her real work as superintendent had just begun. The day after school closed, the state commissioner of education announced that BCPS would have one year to demonstrate substantial improvement in eleven underperforming schools or risk takeover by the state. Although Morris had expected a formal response to stagnant student test scores in Bowen's lowest performing schools, the commissioner's warning received her full attention.

Middleton, a large, once-thriving industrial city that today suffers from high rates of unemployment and poverty, stands at the center of BCPS, a district of 130 schools covering fifty-eight square miles. Most of Middleton's residents are African American or Hispanic, while most residents of the small working-class suburbs that surround the city are white. Morris had arrived in BCPS at a time of relative stability. Her predecessor, an insider who worked his way up through the system, retired after four years in his position. She was careful to take stock of the situation before taking action. She was not usually tentative as an administrator, but her new constituents—even school board members—had warned her against sudden changes. Initially, Morris sought to improve the district's *current operations while systematically learning more about BCPS. She commissioned a study of the district's academic program, visited every school, convened groups of teachers and principals for open discussions, surveyed parents, and courted business leaders. People appreciated meeting her and being heard, but Morris realized that she now needed to act and address the problems of performance and inequity that BCPS faced.*

Some people who spoke to Morris sought reassurance that nothing would change in BCPS, but many others, especially parents and community leaders in center-city Middleton, pointed to achievement gaps of twenty-eight to thirty-three percentage points between minority and white students across the district. They also noted dramatic differences in graduation rates from one high school to another. Although the curriculum technically was uniform throughout the countywide district, schools in the suburbs offered many more Advanced Placement (AP) courses and specialized areas of study in fields such as engineering or environmental studies. Also, teachers in the city schools often transferred to the suburbs. Some said that these teachers changed schools because they wanted to work with more successful students, but the teachers claimed that schools in Middleton often had poor principals who ran dysfunctional schools.

Morris knew that her greatest challenge was to see that all students could attend first-rate schools, but she wasn't sure how to achieve excellence in every school. Many principals, including some in Middleton, were outstanding. But those same successful principals often complained that central office administrators buried them in useless paperwork and could not help them solve the simplest problems. It seemed to Morris that if the principal could have a greater say in key decisions, students would probably benefit. Yet it also appeared that the most successful principals continued to get more and more resources, sometimes at the expense of their less-successful peers. Giving the best principals more autonomy might inadvertently mean that the least effective schools would fall further behind.

Alternatively, Morris might take steps to see that the central office responded to and met the needs of all principals—the best as well as those who struggled. That would call for breaking down the isolating silos

among the departments of the central office, firing ineffective adminis-
trators, and hiring or promoting others. If the district could ensure that
every school would get its fair share of resources and attention, then all
principals could be held to high standards. Taking this approach, how-
ever, was also fraught with challenges. If central office did not deliver,
then the best principals would create work-arounds, further exacerbating
inequitable distribution of resources across schools. Under this scenario,
Morris was sure principals in suburban schools would win a greater share
than the other principals.

Thinking about the commissioner's warning, Morris considered two
approaches that might work for BCPS—giving principals more auton-
omy or ensuring that the central office would provide the support princi-
pals needed—though surely there were others. Despite her determination
to move ahead immediately, she suspected that she would lose sleep in
deciding just what path to take.

Jackie Morris is not a real person, but her circumstances and dilemma
certainly are. Across the United States, superintendents, school
boards, policy makers, and education reformers weigh the advantages
and disadvantages of centralization and decentralization in school
management. Will students benefit more from a system of even-
handed, standardized treatment for all schools, where central office
administrators make key decisions about curriculum, pedagogy, the
budget, and staffing? Or would students be better served by a system
that grants schools broad autonomy, either conditionally or uncon-
ditionally, to decide how to run their school? Or should districts like
Bowen adopt an approach that includes elements of each? And, if so,
how best might they be combined?

School officials who contemplate these questions reach different conclusions. For example, in the aftermath of the devastation
caused by Hurricane Katrina, New Orleans moved sharply toward
decentralization by adopting a portfolio model of management that
converted all schools to charter status. In a less radical reform, Philadelphia created a tiered-autonomy policy, allowing certain successful

and experienced principals to design their own education program and manage all of their school's operations. Other principals were entitled to the same level of autonomy coupled with extensive support from central office administrators, while Philadelphia's central office retained full control of another group, designated intervention schools.

While these districts decentralize and move to expand autonomy for schools, others pursue greater consistency across schools. For example, in Winston-Salem, where many magnet schools offer varied programs and an open enrollment system allows students to attend any school, officials express concern that the decentralized approach has led to inequity among schools.[1] After a careful study of the school district, administrators found significant discrepancies among schools in resources, funding, and technology, and they are now working to address the inconsistencies. Similarly, in Jefferson County, Kentucky (Louisville), the state education commissioner criticized the district for creating two systems with very different expectations and outcomes, a situation that he called "academic apartheid."[2] District leaders have responded with a new strategic plan that calls for developing a "coordinated system" for both professional development and student support while institutionalizing and monitoring best instructional practices.[3] Perhaps most interesting is the trend of charter school management organizations to centralize decisions and build out "home offices" as they scale up.[4] For example, KIPP, which has 162 charter schools in twenty states, has begun to make "selective investments in standardization" of school accountability frameworks and leadership pipelines. According to KIPP, these standardized practices enable the system of charter schools to "operate effectively and efficiently."[5]

THE MISSION OF LARGE URBAN SCHOOL DISTRICTS

Large, urban school districts in the United States are expected to play a special role in this nation's effort to ensure racial, social, and economic equity. Although they represent only a small fraction of all school districts in the United States, they serve vast numbers of students, many with great needs. Large proportions of urban students live in poverty, experience racism, encounter violence, are identified for special education, and are learning English as a second language. For example, the sixty-seven school systems that have been identified by the Council of Great City Schools as large urban school districts educate nearly seven million students—one of every seven children in the United States.[6] These same large districts also enroll 24 percent of all Hispanic students in the country, 28 percent of African American students, and 25 percent of English language learners.[7]

However, most of these districts have had, at best, modest success in serving students in all their schools. In many we see large gaps in achievement between minority and majority students. Schools that serve middle-class students tend to have more resources, more stability, and more experienced teachers and principals than schools that serve low-income students.[8] All districts can point to a small number of schools that effectively serve low-income students, but these often are islands of excellence; there is little evidence that the success of those schools can easily be scaled up.[9] Thus, the most important and motivating mission for the leaders of large, urban districts is to effectively serve all students so that they have equal opportunities and achieve consistent success.

It is this mission of urban education that motivated our study about the relationship between the central office and the schools. Most superintendents agree that a key role of the central office is to support the schools. Yet, superintendents (or principals, for that matter) often don't see eye-to-eye about what level of support is called for or what the change would entail. The debate is ongoing: Where should decisions be made, in schools or at the central office? Where does the greater capacity to improve performance exist, at the central office or in the schools? At which level of the system should more authority rest, at the top or at the bottom? What approach to decision making would lead to higher performance across all schools, centralized or decentralized? We sought to address these questions as problems of practice. Our goal was to offer a close and nuanced exploration of how districts that are recognized for their improvement and success structure this relationship.

THE ROLE OF THE PUBLIC EDUCATION LEADERSHIP PROJECT

This book grows out of research we undertook as part of Harvard University's Public Education Leadership Project (PELP). When PELP launched in 2003, school districts were only beginning to understand the implications of the federal No Child Left Behind Act of 2001 (NCLB). The stated goal of NCLB was that all public school students reach proficiency, as measured by standardized tests, by the end of the 2013–2014 school year. Reformers who championed the law assumed that if states set high standards and held schools accountable to those standards, student performance would improve. States then selected tests and administered them each year in order to determine if schools met Adequate Yearly Progress (AYP). Schools that did not meet AYP faced a series of sanctions that could eventually lead to state takeover. It was in this context that PELP began—first as a pilot project and then as an ongoing initiative—to better understand how school districts could improve performance.

PELP was organized as a joint venture between Harvard Business School (HBS) and the Harvard Graduate School of Education (HGSE). The theory behind the collaboration was that each school would bring specialized expertise to the problems of practice in U.S. public education, HBS contributing a broad understanding of management and HGSE bringing expertise in education. Together they would generate new knowledge about how to manage school systems. A core group of faculty members from both schools set the mission of PELP: *to make a substantial difference in public education by improving the management and leadership competencies and practices of public education leaders.* In pursuing that mission, PELP partnered with eight urban school districts from across the country to conduct practice-based research, develop teaching case studies, and sponsor a summer institute where urban district leadership teams could learn more about the principles of management and leadership in education.

Our annual, six-day summer institute has been the core of PELP's collaborative work with school districts. Districts attend in leadership teams composed of senior central office leaders, principals, union leaders, board members, and others. Each team selects a strategic problem of practice that becomes the focus of their work with PELP facilitators and faculty. During the week, we complement facilitated team sessions with plenary case discussions and simulations designed to support teams in managing, leading, and developing coherent organizational systems that will lead to better learning for all students. To conclude the institute, PELP pairs districts to share their work in order to develop sustainable relationships and networks well after the institute ends.

Through collaborating with partner districts, we at PELP have gained a number of insights about managing large urban school districts. We have confirmed that the central office does matter and is important in achieving excellence across all schools. We have also learned that success requires a districtwide strategy that focuses on improving instruction in the classroom and that the district is key in creating such a plan, developing capacity to implement it with fidelity, monitoring performance, and holding people accountable for results. Finally, we developed a conceptual tool, the Coherence Framework, to help districts identify the organizational elements and environmental factors that might facilitate or impede a strategy for improvement.

These early findings provided the foundation for our understanding of how to manage large urban school districts. They also generated more questions from our district partners. District leaders still found that one of the greatest challenges was executing a strategy across schools that had very different needs, capacities, and communities. The PELP Coherence Framework identified the parts of the system and asserted that those parts should be "coherent," but it did not explain what a productive relationship between the parts looked like or how to achieve coherence. Districts found it especially challenging to manage the relationship between the central office and the schools.

The superintendents agreed that the central office–schools relationship was critical to improving performance. Yet, their assumptions and expectations about what that relationship should be differed. Some believed that the balance of decisions should tip toward schools and that principals should have more authority over key decisions that affected them. Others argued that only the central office was in a position to distribute resources equitably and ensure a consistent standard of excellence across schools. Given this current, pressing challenge described by our district partners, we decided to investigate it further.

We chose to visit and study five districts that all were recognized for their success and improvement yet approached the central office–schools relationship differently. We believed that comparing and contrasting the approaches would shed light on which interactions between the central office and the schools mattered most. We also wondered whether one approach would be more effective than others. With these goals in mind, we reviewed research about central office–schools relationships to build a foundation for our study.

WHAT RESEARCH TELLS US ABOUT CENTRAL OFFICE–SCHOOLS RELATIONSHIPS

As we planned our research, we looked for other studies that focus on the relationship between the central office and the schools, especially in large, urban districts. Although a good deal of research exists about either school leadership or central office management, we were surprised at how few studies focus on the intersection between the two. However, those who have studied this relationship report that a basic tension exists between the priorities of administrators in the central office and those in the schools.[10] They find that principals and local school communities push for greater freedom to set their own priorities and allocate resources in response to their school's identified needs, while district administrators, who bear responsibility for maintaining equity across schools and ensuring that the public's money is well spent, are reluctant to relinquish their formal authority to make key decisions.

Interestingly, policy makers appear to influence whether districts favor the central office or the schools in these relationships. For example, Johnson and Chrispeels suggest that federal and state accountability mandates, especially No Child Left Behind, have "placed the district at the forefront" by holding it responsible for improving teaching and learning.[11] In contrast, Steinberg points to the effects of a different U.S. federal policy—Race to the Top (RTTT)—which "gave priority to states that not only expanded the number of authorized charter schools but also instituted a broader reform strategy enabling local school districts to operate autonomous public, non-charter schools."[12] Therefore, recent policies have influenced how districts approach the central office–schools relationship, though not in the same direction. Some encourage giving more control to the district, others to the schools.

Recognizing that administrators in both the central office and the schools have legitimate, though sometimes divergent, concerns as they work to serve students, researchers and policy makers widely agree that the central office–schools relationship should be coordinated, or "coherent." Chrispeels, Burke, Johnson, and Daly report that "high levels of student achievement are possible when schools and the district act as coordinated units of change."[13] Honig, whose research focused on the role of the central office in improving teaching and learning, reached similar conclusions.[14] Based on these and similar findings, it seems essential that those in the central office and in the schools know what authority or responsibility each has, how that authority can be exercised, and what mutual accommodations should be made in the process.

Despite overall agreement about the importance of achieving coordination and clarity in central office–schools relationships, scholars acknowledge that doing so is not simple and that district practices, even those judged to be coordinated or coherent, remain complex. Honig and Hatch recommend conceiving of coherence not as "an objective alignment" but as a "dynamic process" that "involves schools and school district central offices working together" to craft or continually negotiate the fit between external demands and schools' own goals and strategies.[15] Thompson, Sykes, and Skrla, who provide an informative overview of the process involved in reconciling competing interests between the district and the schools, conclude that coordination is achieved through a set of ongoing, dynamic processes that create balance, differentiation, legitimacy, and trust.[16]

Conceptually, these ideas make sense, but how do they play out in practice, especially in large districts, where ongoing accommodations are difficult to predict and manage? Supovitz's 2006 longitudinal case study of Duval County, Florida, provides an unusually detailed analysis of how that district managed its central office–schools relationships.[17] Supovitz documents the district's efforts to enact "a unifying vision of instructional quality while maintaining some level of local flexibility" and to shift the central office from its traditional, managerial role to one of support for the schools.[18] He describes various instances when both the central office and the schools exercise some control over decisions that affect teaching and learning: "In the more centralized approaches, the district builds or adopts a particular conception of instructional quality. In the more decentralized approaches, the instructional vision may emanate from school faculties, but the district develops and implements a particular process for engaging school faculties in the challenges of instructional improvement."[19] It is through such processes, Supovitz argues, that "seemingly contradictory and opposing ideas [that] butt up against each other . . . are brought into harmony."[20] These findings suggest that those working in central offices and schools would benefit from descriptive studies that compare how and with what success other districts manage, and perhaps reconcile, these competing interests.

Given the pressure of accountability, some researchers have tried to determine what effects different approaches to central office–schools relationships have on student achievement. However, this line of research is inconclusive. Ouchi makes the strongest claims for the benefits of granting schools full autonomy.[21] He compared three districts that had many years of experience with decentralized schooling (Edmonton, Alberta, Canada; Seattle; and Houston) with three other districts that had once adopted decentralized management but subsequently reverted to centralized control (New York, Los Angeles, and Chicago). Acknowledging that his sample was small and the evidence fragmentary, Ouchi still concludes that decentralized districts outperform centralized districts "both in overall student performance and in reducing achievement gaps between racial groups."[22] Steinberg, however, challenges Ouchi's findings because he fails to provide evidence of a direct effect of school-based autonomy on student performance.[23] Other researchers point to students' academic success in districts that operate with centralized approaches to management, such as Montgomery County, Maryland, and San Diego.[24] Meanwhile, Abdulkadiroglu and colleagues conducted a study of autonomous (pilot) schools within Boston and found mixed effects on student achievement in math and reading.[25] Therefore, the final answer is not yet in on the question of whether centralized or decentralized management of schools is more effective.

For a number of important reasons, researchers may never be able to say with confidence which model is superior. First, because many factors influence student achievement, it is difficult, if not impossible, to attribute changes in students' test scores to a management model, even a basic one. Second, even if the approaches have the same label— decentralization or centralization—they are unlikely to be the same. Third, time matters. The stream of school improvement is always moving as districts adopt new policies and priorities, whether on their own or in response to state or federal mandates. Even if researchers set out to conduct simultaneous longitudinal studies, the districts in their sample would inevitably be at different points of development when the study began, which would affect how findings could be interpreted.

Although it may not be possible to assess the effects of different management models on student achievement, there is still much to be learned about what is involved in coordinating central office–schools relationships. This understudied topic is of great importance in determining students' opportunities to learn.

COHERENCE AND THE COHERENCE FRAMEWORK

Coherence, congruence, and *alignment* are terms often used to describe what organizations should strive for in their efforts to reach high performance. For the most part, people intuitively understand why this is important. When a high degree of coherence exists, people agree on the work that needs to be done in order to achieve strategic goals, what resources support that work, and which systems and structures facilitate it. Unfortunately, the education literature provides few examples to illustrate our intuitive understanding of coherence. The complexity of urban districts makes it difficult to analyze how organizational elements reinforce or hamper the district's improvement strategy. Those in the central office interact with scores of schools, and each relationship may be more or less coherent than others.

In business, numerous books, articles, trainings, and blogs are dedicated to helping managers ensure that work on the ground supports strategic goals. In the business literature, attention to the link between coherence and organizational performance is decades old. In their classic *In Search for Excellence*, Peters and Waterman describe characteristics of high performing organizations to illustrate their 7-S model, one of the first management theories to assert that all the elements of an organization—strategy, systems, structure, skills, style, staff, and shared values—should work harmoniously to achieve excellence.[26] Tushman and O'Reilly advanced these ideas with their congruence model, which proposes that organizations must align critical tasks, people, formal organizational structures, and culture with strategic intent to reach high performance.[27] Importantly, they also describe how the environment shapes business strategy and organizational elements. In business, strategy is usually developed in response to external forces such as competitors, suppliers, customers, and economic conditions. Achieving coherence or congruence in the business world means aligning the strategy and organizational elements with the environmental conditions of success.

When PELP researchers began to write teaching cases about how districts managed their schools, they quickly saw the relevance of the congruence model—with one key caveat. In education, the environment can often distract or impede districts from pursuing their core mission of improving student outcomes. Thus, when the PELP team members adapted the congruence model to create their Coherence Framework, they placed the Instructional Core in the center to remind everyone that what really matters happens in the classroom with the interaction of teachers, students, and rich content.[28]

FIGURE I.1   PELP coherence framework

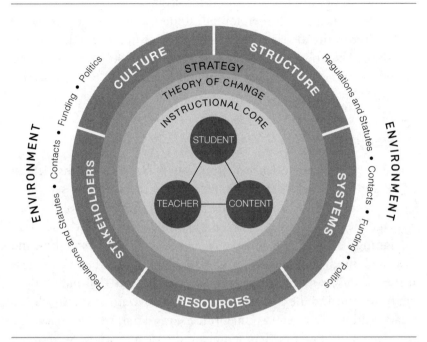

Surrounding the Instructional Core are factors that affect what happens in the classroom—the environment, theory of change, strategy, systems, structures, stakeholders, resources, and culture (see figure I.1). The fundamental idea is that, when all those components function together coherently, the system works well, teachers and students succeed in the Instructional Core, and the district can achieve its mission.

Over the years, district leaders told us that the Coherence Framework was a useful tool for developing strategy and analyzing organizational systems. However, they struggled to understand how it could help them manage diverse schools for consistent, sustained improvement. According to our district partners, the challenge of coherence centers on the relationship between the central office and the schools and how to translate their intuitive understanding of coherence into ongoing practices and day-to-day interactions.

We were interested, therefore, in understanding what coherence looked like in the districts' approaches to central office–schools relationships. The Coherence Framework served as a tool for focusing our attention on the key components and for examining the relationships among them.

THE STUDY

Based on what we had learned from our partner school districts in PELP and informed by the relevant research literature, we set out to understand, analyze, and describe how large, urban school districts manage their relationship between the central office and the schools. Designing a study that would provide both broad understanding and practical insights and lessons was challenging, given the size of these districts, the many political and economic factors that define their environment, and the complexity of the issue of central office–schools relationships. We faced two major decisions. First, we had to select a manageable and appropriate sample of districts to study. Second, we had to decide how to define the elements of the central office–schools relationship as we collected data in each district. (See the appendix for the study's research methods.)

Although it's always possible to learn from failure, we decided to focus on what works. Therefore, we chose a set of districts that were recognized for their success and/or steady improvement. In identifying districts that arguably had achieved or were achieving success, we began by creating a list of finalists or winners of the Broad Prize for Urban Education as well as other districts cited by experts and the media for their improvement. It's necessary to emphasize that we sought to understand one important aspect of these districts' practice: their central office–schools relationships. We were not trying to explain how the "best" districts succeeded. However, we did not ignore performance. We took seriously evidence about student learning, especially about the gaps in academic achievement between majority and minority subgroups. But we realized from prior research that it would be irresponsible to claim that a straight arrow can be drawn between one factor of a school district's managerial practice and student achievement. Many other factors—funding, public support of public education, state standards, preparation of teachers, quality of principals, and the well-being of families—affect teaching and learning. However, we assumed that district officials choose their approach to managing schools believing that it will contribute to improved student achievement. Therefore, we wanted to understand how their approaches work.

In addition to studying districts recognized for their progress and accomplishments, we wanted to be sure that we had variation within our sample in the districts' approaches, ranging from centralization to decentralization. Therefore, we began by selecting Montgomery County and Baltimore City school districts, both participants in PELP. Both had made impressive progress in various indicators of success (for example, graduation rates, test scores, attendance, and closing the achievement gap), yet they relied on very different beliefs to guide their practice. Montgomery County had long pursued centralized management practices, while Baltimore City had recently turned sharply toward decentralization. We then added three non-PELP districts to our sample: Aldine, Texas, and Long Beach, California, which were widely known for being centralized, and Charlotte-Mecklenburg in North Carolina, which had over time moved from centralized to decentralized practices.

Our overall research question was, *How do these five districts manage the relationship between their central office and their schools?* Also, we sought to learn whether districts relied on consistently centralized or decentralized approaches in making the key decisions that affected student learning. In our summer institute we had presented nine district teams (eight members each) with a continuum running from centralized to decentralized management. We asked each person to place a dot on the continuum noting where they thought their district fell on five key decisions—curriculum, staffing, budget, governance, and schedules (see figures I.2–I.5). We found that participants within a district generally agreed about where their district belonged on the continuum—that is, their eight dots clustered near one point on the continuum. Notably,

FIGURE I.2   Where are budgeting decisions made?

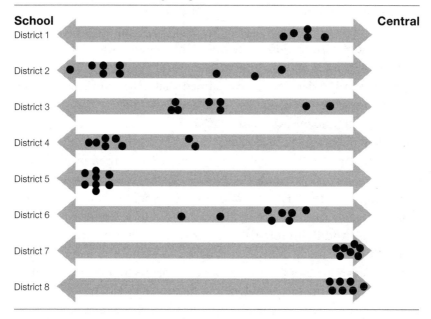

FIGURE I.3   Where are academic programming decisions made?

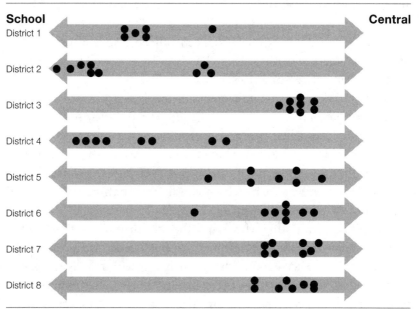

FIGURE I.4   Where are staffing decisions made?

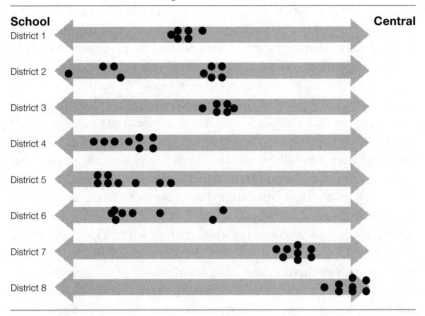

FIGURE I.5   Where are decisions made, overall?

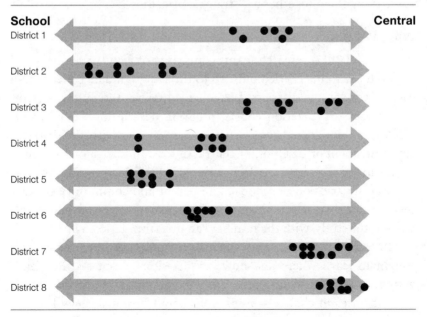

however, those clusters did not align for all decisions. That is, partic- ipants did not report that their districts always relied on the same approach for different decisions. This suggested that districts might adopt a mix-and-match approach and that it would be worthwhile to study how the districts allocated responsibility for several key decisions.

We then had to decide which decisions to study, given that researchers and reformers have generated similar, lengthy lists of the functions that autonomous schools should control.[29] We looked closely at the autonomies granted to the pilot schools in Boston, since they had been formally negotiated by teachers and administrators, had been in place since 1995, and had served as the model for other large, urban districts, including Los Angeles.[30] These autonomies included staffing; budget; curriculum, instruction, and assessment; schedules; and governance. Informal inquiry with PELP participants convinced us that several of these decisions—staffing, budget, and curriculum, instruction, and assessment—were of most importance to both the central office and the schools and were thought to have the greatest effect on the instructional core. We then summarized these key decisions as staffing, budgeting, and the academic program, identifying them together as "strategic priorities."

What We Did

In 2011 and 2012, research teams comprised of faculty members and research assistants carried out two to three days of data collection in each of the sample districts. We collected relevant documents (stra- tegic plans, organization charts, program descriptions, key memo- randa) and conducted semistructured interviews with the district's superintendent or CEO; other central office administrators responsi- ble for major functions, such as curriculum and instruction, finance, staffing, supervision of schools, and parent and community engage- ment; and a diverse sample of principals. We interviewed 63 individ- uals for the study, with the number ranging from 12 to 15 per district.

In our interviews and analysis of relevant documents, we sought to learn where and how key decisions about staffing, bud- geting, and the academic program were made. We wanted to know what theories of change—predictions about how a strategy leads to improvement—guided a district's approach. We tried to identify how local approaches to central office–schools management affected different schools, especially those serving high-income and low-income communities. We wanted to understand whether those we interviewed offered consistent assessments of their district's practices. What tensions were apparent at different places in the district's organization, given their management strategy, systems, and structures? What roles proved to be important in advancing or inhibiting progress in implementing their strategy? How did the district's organizational culture create opportunities and constraints for improvement? How did the district's external environment—its economic, legal, social, and political context—affect what was expected or possible? We pursued these questions directly through questions and indirectly by probing for examples and interpretations. (Our interview protocols and methodology are included in the appendix.)

We transcribed all interviews and then coded them using a set of codes that emerged from our professional knowledge and experience, the literature we reviewed, and the interviews themselves. We then spent several months analyzing our data, exchanging memos about emergent findings, and developing our understanding of organizational coherence based on these districts' approaches.

Although we conducted intensive interviews with a wide range of respondents in five districts, our study has limitations. It is not longitudinal, and therefore we cannot present findings about change over time or about the effects of a management practice on student performance. Data collection took place during just one year, and in every district we solicited opinions, interpretations, and examples over the course of only a few days. We also interviewed a small proportion of the principals in each school district. We recognize the constraints this presents as we interpret and explain what we learned. Moreover, the districts were at different points in the superintendents' tenure and in the development in their particular approaches—some well established, others relatively new. Therefore, we're careful not to draw conclusive comparisons across districts. However, we can comment on how this group of districts dealt with opportunities and challenges at different points along the way.

What We Found

School districts are complex organizations. Teachers, principals, and central office administrators interact in countless ways, all shaped by a web of political, legal, and historical factors. Our findings reflect this complexity. They are grounded in the everyday experiences of central office administrators and principals as they made key decisions about budgeting, staffing, and the academic program. Here we present a preview of our main findings. Each chapter builds on these using examples and quotations from those we interviewed.

Our key finding directly addresses the long debate about which approach to managing central office–schools relationships—centralization or decentralization—is best. Currently, policy and practice seem to favor pushing decisions out to the schools, though we expect that this trend eventually will reverse. We learned that the five districts were able to show improvement using very different organizational approaches. The choices the districts made about the basic building blocks of their strategy—what we call the *strategic priorities* of academic programing, budgeting, and staffing—varied widely, but all showed success in some way. For example, on one hand, Aldine, Long Beach, and Montgomery County would be seen by most to rely on centralization. Compared with many other districts, each had, in varying degrees, granted relatively less autonomy to the schools for key decisions about academic programing, budgeting, and staffing. Yet all three had achieved national recognition for success in educating their students. On the other hand, Baltimore and Charlotte-Mecklenburg followed a largely decentralized approach, pushing significant decision-making rights and responsibility for the same three strategic priorities out to their principals. These two districts had also received recognition for success and improvement.

What mattered most was achieving coherence, and we found that districts could do that while relying on a theory of change based on either centralization or decentralization. The essential ingredient to improvement was whether a district could effectively implement whatever theory of change it chose.

One key to achieving coherence was establishing mutually supportive relationships and trust between the central office and the schools. However, we discovered that district leaders often overlook the process of building and sustaining trust, which occurs through particular decisions and interactions over a long period of time. For example, if a new math curriculum is recommended or mandated, principals must be convinced that it is of a higher quality than current offerings and that the central office will provide promised support for teachers as it is implemented.

Finally, we found that two elements of the Coherence Framework—the environment and culture—were critical but often overlooked aspects of the central office–schools relationships. These districts' experiences demonstrated that the organizational culture of a district could be a barrier to or an enabler of efforts to improve performance. If a district is intentional about making strategic choices to achieve coherence, then it is likely that, as they are enacted, those choices will change the culture of the district. Similarly, the external environment can serve as an enabler if leaders can nimbly and wisely develop strategies to respond to and sometimes influence these regulatory, contractual, financial, and political forces that surround them.

WHAT YOU CAN EXPECT IN READING THIS BOOK

Our aim was to write a book that would be useful to practitioners. Therefore, we rely heavily on the stories, quotations, and examples from the people we interviewed in order to understand the broader elements of the district's beliefs, strategy, and practices. We did this by focusing on the problem of practice of managing the relationship between the central office and the schools, which PELP districts had identified as critical to their current efforts to improve student learning. Our data, analysis, and suggestions radiate from this theme, with the Coherence Framework serving as a guide for our inquiry. At the end of each chapter we offer practical advice with "Lessons for Practice," actionable takeaways drawn from the main findings of each chapter.

ONE

Five Districts in Search of Improvement

In this chapter we introduce the districts in our study in order to situate the findings and discussion that follow. It is important to know, for example, that Andrés Alonso was the seventh Baltimore superintendent in ten years when considering our findings about the importance of culture in the central office–schools relationship. Indeed, when we visited the five school districts over one year, they were in different stages of change, and each served a unique community. Some districts had a long history of success, and others were just a few years into showing improved performance. The superintendents had a wide range of experiences and tenures. Montgomery County superintendent Josh Starr was finishing his first year in that position, while Superintendent Chris Steinhauoor had led Long Beach for nearly a decade. Approaches to managing the central office–school relationship also differed. Aldine was resolutely centralized in its approach; Charlotte-Mecklenburg was actively trying to give schools more autonomy. Despite these differences, all faced the common challenge of managing many schools with diverse needs in order to achieve consistent, high performance across their systems.

We begin with vignettes about each of the districts, focusing on the community served, leadership, key issues, and influential contextual factors. The chapter concludes with an overview of some commonalities among the districts, including size, governance, and performance. The chapter has a dual purpose. The first is to give enough background so that the reader will understand how our data and the findings that emerged were situated within a particular context during a specific time. The second is to suggest how that context might have influenced what we discovered in our interviews of superintendents, central office administrators, and principals.

ALDINE INDEPENDENT SCHOOL DISTRICT

The Aldine, Texas, community looked very different thirty years ago than it does today. In the late 1970s, over 75 percent of students were white.[1] A court desegregation order in 1978 forced the district to redraw its boundaries so that no school had more than 30 percent black students.[2] A subsequent increase of black students diversified the school system into the 1980s. Through the 1990s Aldine experienced rapid growth in its Hispanic and low-income student population so that by 2005 most students were Hispanic from low-income communities. In 2011 Aldine served working-class and low-income communities on the northern fringe of Houston: 66 percent identified as Hispanic and 28 percent as African American, and 85 percent qualified for a free and reduced-price lunch. Nearly one-third of the students had limited English proficiency.

Despite rapid changes in its student population over the years, the district's governance and senior leadership have remained remarkably stable. As of 2011, all board members had at least five years' experience in that role, and two had served for more than twenty years. The stability in the elected board was apparent in the consistency in board policy, mission, strategy, and district leadership. Over thirty years there had been only four superintendents, all of whom were once teachers or administrators in Aldine. Wanda Bamberg became superintendent in May 2007 after having worked in the district for twenty-five years as a teacher, director of middle school language arts, and assistant superintendent of curriculum and instruction.

The district was organized into five preK–12 feeder systems called "verticals," a structure that had been in place since 1995. Each vertical included three to seven elementary schools, two or three middle schools and junior highs, and one large comprehensive high school. Students from the elementary schools fed into the middle schools and junior highs along the vertical and then into the one high school. An area superintendent oversaw each vertical system and was responsible for hiring and evaluating principals, monitoring school performance, communicating district initiatives, and organizing vertical-wide meetings of principals and professional development.

Texas does not permit collective bargaining for public employees. However, three local teacher associations operated in the district, offering teachers professional advice, insurance, and networking opportunities. The largest and most active of these was the Aldine American Federation of Teachers (AAFT), with approximately eight hundred members. During our research, the district and AAFT had an accommodating relationship, though there had been contentious disagreements in the past.

Leaders in Aldine often referred to the "Aldine Way," a culture including beliefs that all students can reach proficiency if teachers get the support they need to make it happen and are held accountable. The sway of the state test and accountability system was strong in Aldine, and the district based its instructional expectations almost entirely on the Texas test. At the time of our visit, the leaders in Aldine were most concerned about a new, more challenging state test being implemented the following year. They expected to see a dip in test scores, which would then begin to improve over time.

BALTIMORE CITY PUBLIC SCHOOLS

After decades of decline, dysfunction, and poor performance, Baltimore in 2012 was five years into a districtwide turnaround process led by Andrés Alonso. For nearly five decades, the downward trajectory of the school system mirrored that of the city. Once the nation's sixth-largest city, Baltimore's population declined for six straight decades, losing more than 300,000 residents between 1950 and 2010 due to work relocation and suburban migration. As the city's industrial economy shifted from shipping, steel, and auto manufacturing to services, few jobs were available for the residents of Baltimore, most of whom were black. Unemployment soared, buildings and homes were left vacant or in disrepair, and the school system struggled to consolidate schools and successfully educate a greater proportion of low-income students.

When Alonso took over in 2007, the system was in crisis. The district had seen seven superintendents in ten years and enrollment had steadily declined, down by 30,000 students since 1995. Since the early 2000s no grade level had ever made AYP under NCLB.[3] In 2007 only 48 percent of students in grades 3–8 were proficient in math and 57 percent proficient in reading. The graduation rate was 60 percent.[4] Because of its chronically poor performance and history of mismanagement, Baltimore was governed by a special ten-member board jointly appointed by the Baltimore mayor and Maryland governor, a structure that had been in place since 1997.

When Alonso arrived, he began to shift decision making and resources away from the central office and toward the schools, granting principals and teachers much more control over decisions in academic programming, budgeting, and staffing. Alonso's past experiences as a special education teacher and deputy chancellor for the New York City Department of Education informed his work. He established Fair Student Funding, which assigned a base amount of funding to students that followed them no matter what school they attended in the city. At the same time, he shifted control of budgets to schools; within two years principals went from controlling 3 percent of their budgets to controlling roughly 80 percent. And he introduced a new network structure in which schools received support from a team of five to eight specialists coordinated by a lead facilitator. Each principal was also assigned an executive director, who provided coaching and evaluated the principal.

The district had an active teachers union, the Baltimore Teachers Union (BTU), an affiliate of the American Federation of Teachers (AFT), representing teachers, related service providers, and support staff.[5] In the fall of 2010, Baltimore City Schools and BTU signed a landmark contract that replaced the traditional "steps and lanes" pay scale with a career ladder that was tied to teachers' performance. The contract established four self-paced career pathways—standard, professional, model, and lead—that teachers could progress through by earning "achievement units" and passing a review by a panel of peers.[6]

At the time of our visit, there was a sense of progress and accomplishment among the central office administrators and principals in Baltimore. At the same time, many also acknowledged that Baltimore remained an underperforming urban school district and that the hardest work lay ahead. The system, which had created a safer learning environment with fewer disruptions and less violence, also had seen students make academic gains. However, there were serious concerns about the capacity in both the central office and the schools to deliver rigorous curriculum and instruction in the years ahead.

CHARLOTTE-MECKLENBURG SCHOOLS

Over the last three decades, Charlotte's population has more than doubled as it became a major financial center in the United States. With the city's population approaching 800,000 and a surrounding metropolitan area of more than 2 million, Charlotte has experienced periods of rapid growth and change in its school system.[7] When we visited Charlotte-Mecklenburg in the spring of 2011, the district was about to change leaders. The superintendent at the time, Peter Gorman, announced his resignation just a few months after we completed our interviews and just before the district was awarded the Broad Prize for Urban Education, a $1 million prize given annually to the top-performing and most-improved urban school districts in the nation.

When he became superintendent in 2006, Gorman took over the state's largest school system during a challenging time. His predecessors, Eric Smith (1996–2002) and James Pughsley (2002–2005), had spent nearly a decade trying to establish more consistent practices across the 160 schools in the district. Teachers in all schools were expected to use the same curricula and follow similar sequencing of topics. Decision making about curriculum and instruction shifted to central office specialists. Hiring procedures were standardized. At the time, suburban parents were upset about the student assignment system and overcrowded schools, the business community criticized the district's poor high school performance, and serious racial conflicts divided the city. Also, the school board was known to be dysfunctional and split.[8] The nine-member elected board included three at-large members and six members representing various regions, an arrangement that exacerbated divides, particularly among members representing communities in the city and their suburban counterparts. When the board appointed Gorman, it told him to get everyone working together, to improve the image of the district, and to restructure decision making so that principals would have more authority.[9]

Gorman set an ambitious agenda. Prior to his arrival, principals were required to abide by a comprehensive list of "nonnegotiables." One of Gorman's first steps was to grant successful principals "Freedom and Flexibility" from this list. Gorman and his team also implemented the Strategic Staffing Initiative to give principals of low performing schools more control over staffing. In order to further decentralize the district, officials split the district into five zones.[10]

However, the command-and-control culture fostered under two previous superintendents remained strong. Although Gorman took steps to decentralize decision making, principals still did not have full control over whom they hired or how they spent money. Budget cuts compelled the central office to take more control over the placement and transfer of teachers, and the district still operated largely on a relational basis with the central office staff driving those relationships. In addition, the state distributed funding in staffing units, not dollars, so principals had little discretionary funds for their schools.

At the time of our visit, the schools were organized into five zones, each led by a zone superintendent. Introduced in June 2010, the zones replaced seven "learning communities" that Gorman had originally created in the 2007–2008 school year "to decentralize the district."[11] The zones were primarily regional, although all the schools qualifying for Title I designation (with roughly 75 percent or more of their students qualifying for free and reduced-price lunch) were grouped into two zones—one for elementary schools and another for middle and high schools—that were located in the center of the city.

By 2010 the student assignment process established in 2002 had essentially desegregated the Charlotte-Mecklenburg schools. Budget cuts forced school closures, which disproportionately impacted schools that served high proportions of low-income and minority students.[12] Local and state NAACP leaders protested, demanded an independent audit of the district's 2011–2012 budget, and filed a civil rights complaint with the U.S. Department of Education.[13] As in Texas, North Carolina teachers cannot bargain collectively, leaving local teachers unions to play a role of service and support. However, state-level union affiliates have considerable political influence in North Carolina, a fact that Gorman realized after he strongly endorsed a controversial statewide performance pay scheme that was heavily criticized by both the local Charlotte-Mecklenburg Association of Educators and the state-level Classroom Teachers' Association of North Carolina.[14] In June 2011 Gorman announced his resignation.[15]

LONG BEACH UNIFIED SCHOOL DISTRICT

Located in Southern California adjacent to Los Angeles, Long Beach had many of the same features we found in Aldine: stable leadership, steadily improving student achievement, and a strong organizational culture. There was an intense sense of community in Long Beach, a belief that all children could learn, and a concentrated focus on instruction that had been refined over more than a decade of using the same instructional system. The superintendent at the time of our visit, Chris Steinhauser, had been in the role since 2002. He was not only a thirty-year veteran in the system as a teacher, principal, and deputy superintendent, but he was also a product of Long Beach schools, having attended K–12 there.

Steinhauser was appointed after the respected ten-year veteran superintendent Carl Cohn retired in 2002. Using a top-down, bottom-up collaborative approach, Cohn introduced major reforms after the community faced a crisis in the 1990s when the city lost 35,000 jobs in two years and was plagued by riots following the 1992 acquittal of the police officers charged in the assault of Rodney King. Recession and slow growth statewide and nationally led to budget shortfalls. In the midst of the turmoil, Cohn formed partnerships with the community, collaborated closely with the school board, and developed a comprehensive standards-based system that included content standards, performance standards, and performance assessments.

When Cohn retired, Steinhauser continued many of Cohn's reforms. He also introduced professional learning communities in the high schools and more professional development opportunities for all teachers. He implemented changes gradually through a process that was intended to strike a balance between central and local control. This approach gave teachers, parents, and community members opportunities to provide feedback and input on proposed changes, which central office administrators responded to and took seriously.

When we visited, work was still being carried out through what Steinhauser called a top-down, bottom-up "family system." Most employees lived in Long Beach and had children attending the schools. Steinhauser gave teachers his home phone number and encouraged them to call him directly to report problems, which they sometimes did. For many years the district had maintained a professional and cooperative relationship with the teachers union, the National Education Association's (NEA) affiliate, and the Teachers Association of Long Beach. Nearly all principals and district leaders had at least a decade of teaching experience in Long Beach. There was an explicit belief that in order to be an administrator in Long Beach, one first had to have taught there. Steinhauser said such teaching experience was important in order to "know the culture of Long Beach." One district administrator reported that over the past five years only two principals had been hired from outside the district. The expectation that a principal had to have substantial teaching experience in the district before becoming an administrator was so strong that one principal who had taught six years in Long Beach spoke to us apologetically about his lack of teaching experience and time there.

In contrast to the other districts we studied, Long Beach organized its schools by level rather than by geography. One assistant superintendent oversaw the elementary and middle/K–8 schools, while another was responsible for high schools. Four directors supported the assistant superintendents in coaching and supervising principals. The assistant superintendents reported directly to Steinhauser.

Like Aldine, Long Beach had a history of stable superintendent leadership and school board membership. Tenure for superintendents averaged about eight years, and, during the last sixty years, only one was appointed from outside the district. The five-member school board also had consistent membership and leadership. All members were elected by geographic area and represented a defined group of elementary, middle, and high schools in their region. The structure enabled members to form long-standing relationships with particular schools and community members.

MONTGOMERY COUNTY PUBLIC SCHOOLS

After ten years of steady leadership by a nationally recognized superintendent, Montgomery County was in the early phases of transition to a new administration when we visited in the winter of 2012. Superintendent Josh Starr had been in his position fewer than six months. (Starr was superintendent in Stamford, Connecticut, from 2005 to 2011.) Prior to his arrival, Montgomery County, the nation's sixteenth-largest school district, had received national recognition for its success in "raising the bar, and closing the gap." Overall student achievement had improved dramatically, and by focusing closely on institutional barriers to academic opportunities for black and Hispanic students, the district had significantly narrowed the achievement gap. It also had achieved the highest graduation rate of the fifty largest school systems in the United States. Weast, who had been superintendent since 1999, received much of the credit for the improvements, which are recounted and analyzed in several case studies and a book.[16]

Although Montgomery County was a wealthy enclave for Democratic-leaning DC professionals, it also served a large population of low-income, mostly Latino/Hispanic and African American students.

In short, Montgomery County was really two districts within one. During his tenure, Weast targeted the use of resources by creating two zones, Red and Green, designating concentrations of poverty and wealth in the district. At the beginning of this initiative, many, but not all, of the Red Zone schools were performing poorly while most of the Green Zone schools were doing well. Weast intentionally redirected resources from the Green Zone schools to the Red Zone schools and achieved impressive improvement in students' performance there.

The district had strong, collaborative relationships with its three employee unions representing teachers, administrators, and support services employees. For example, there was a jointly sponsored peer assistance and review (PAR) program that included nearly all staff members in the district, providing them with support for improvement and, if necessary, due process for dismissal. Teachers participating in PAR were assigned an expert "consulting teacher" who provided intense support by helping plan and model lessons, providing resources, team teaching, performing observations, and eventually conducting the formal evaluation of the teacher. The PAR process was overseen by a joint PAR panel composed of teachers, principals, and leaders of their respective unions.

Montgomery County was governed by a seven-member at-large school board. The board appointed the superintendent and set policies. However, a nine-member county council established the tax rate and approved the overall budget for Montgomery County, including that of the school system. Therefore, the school board only recommended the budget to the county council, which could either reject or approve it. At the time of our visit, the district's 200 schools were organized into six geographic regions, each including 29–37 schools; each region was overseen and supported by a community superintendent.

The Weast era was known for its focus on equity, outcomes, and procedures. Decisions were made through highly participatory and process-driven routines, with the district's three labor unions participating centrally in governance. Binders full of flowcharts and formulas ensured systemwide consistency. Montgomery County followed the Baldrige process with fidelity and is one of the few school districts to win the Malcolm Baldrige award.[17] Weast and his deputy superintendent also implemented a system of close performance monitoring. Principals had to present, disaggregate, and analyze their school performance data in regular meetings with their community superintendent. They were expected to meet districtwide targets or provide an explanation coupled with an action plan for the future.

In general, there was great pride among those working for the Montgomery County Public Schools. Employees often dubbed the district the "GE" or "New York Yankees" of school districts. People were highly motivated as they worked in an environment that was variously described as "results-driven," "outcomes-driven," and a "well-oiled machine." Few policies or practices had changed when we visited during Starr's first year as superintendent. However, administrators talked about recent, increased attention to the tension between outcome-driven accountability and innovating for the sake of learning. Under Starr's leadership the district was beginning to examine how best to meet ambitious targets while allowing for experimentation in classrooms and schools. Starr said that he was "reorienting" the culture of the district from one that concentrated on accountability and monitoring to one of that offered support and encouragement for creative improvement. With that reorientation under way (e.g., the Office of School Performance became the Office of School Improvement and Support), its impact on the culture in Montgomery County was uncertain, although the district's focus on equity, outcomes, and procedures seemed likely to continue with well-calculated support from the district's strong systems and structures.

FIVE AMONG MANY

These are only five of the more than thirteen thousand school districts in the United States.[18] For the purpose of our study, they shared several common features. First, they all faced the challenge of managing a large number of schools serving diverse communities. Each had more than sixty thousand students, the majority being students of color (see table 1.1).

Second, each of the districts operated in a complex political environment. The systems of governance differed somewhat across the

TABLE 1.1   District demographics

DISTRICT	SIZE	NUMBER OF SCHOOLS	AFRICAN AMERICAN	HISPANIC	WHITE	FREE/ REDUCED- PRICE LUNCH
Aldine	61,256	78	28%	67%	3%	80%
Baltimore	82,866	188	89%	2%	8%	73%
Charlotte-Mecklenburg	135,064	160	45%	15%	35%	43%
Long Beach	87,509	93	17%	51%	16%	67%
Montgomery County	139,282	200	23%	21%	40%	26%

five school districts, but four of the five school boards were elected, and only Baltimore had an appointed board (see table 1.2). Providing such an important public good as free K–12 education also meant that the districts had to respond to a diverse group of stakeholders in addition to the school board. All of these districts continuously grappled with issues of race, class, gender, and equity while managing an array of interrelated, often shifting, policies made at the local, state, and federal levels.

Third, each of these districts showed notable improvement over time. For some districts, like Aldine, higher performance meant having higher proportions of students achieve at proficient and advanced levels on the state tests. For others, like Montgomery County, improved performance was apparent in the percentage of students ready for college, as demonstrated by their ACT scores. In Baltimore, rapidly growing graduation and enrollment rates served as evidence of high performance. Charlotte-Mecklenburg narrowed achievement gaps between black and white students in reading and math in all grade levels. Long Beach performed higher than all other comparable districts in California. Aldine, Charlotte-Mecklenburg, and Long Beach all won the Broad Prize (see table 1.3 for a summary of national recognition).

TABLE 1.2 National recognition by districts

DISTRICT	NATIONAL RECOGNITION
Aldine	Broad Prize finalist in 2004, 2005, and 2008; won the Broad Prize in 2009
Baltimore	Received Council of Urban Boards of Education (CUBE) Annual Award for Urban School Board Excellence 2010
Charlotte-Mecklenburg	Broad Prize finalist in 2004 and 2010; won the Broad Prize in 2011
Long Beach	Broad Prize finalist in 2002, 2007, 2008, and 2009; won the Broad Prize in 2003
Montgomery County	Received the Malcolm Baldrige National Quality Award and was a finalist for the Broad Prize in Education in 2010; recognized for highest graduation rate of the fifty largest school systems in the United States

TABLE 1.3 Governance characteristics of districts

DISTRICT	BOARD SIZE	ELECTED/APPOINTED
Aldine	7 members	Elected, at-large
Baltimore	10 members	Jointly appointed by Baltimore Mayor and Maryland Governor
Charlotte-Mecklenburg	9 members	Elected, three at-large members and six district representatives
Long Beach	5 members	Elected by geographic area
Montgomery County	7 members	Elected, at-large

Finally, each of the districts took an intentional approach to managing its schools and had a strongly held belief about how that approach affected, or would affect, performance. The superintendents in Baltimore and Charlotte-Mecklenburg predicted that greater autonomy for the schools would lead to improvement. Leaders in Aldine, Long Beach, and Montgomery County believed that the central office should have more say than school leaders in decisions about budgeting, staffing, and the academic program.

TWO

Starting with Strategy

Ideally, everything that district leaders do flows from their commitment to improve what happens with every teacher, for every child, in every classroom. But the organizational distance between the central office and the classroom is often vast, and even a superintendent with abundant formal authority cannot control what actually happens for children day to day. Also, within any large school district, students' interests and needs vary widely across many diverse communities. What works in one school may not work across town. Still, the central office is responsible for serving all children in all schools. Long Beach superintendent Chris Steinhauser framed the challenge this way: "How do you implement reform of the system where, regardless of where the teacher comes in, that teacher will have success?"

Faced with this responsibility, district officials in large, urban systems typically devise and implement a *strategy* for improving teaching and learning in all schools, especially those that have failed to serve their students in the past. That strategy is composed of a set of carefully selected actions and activities, all designed to work in concert to achieve the district's goals for improvement. For example, in a district where school officials seek to equalize learning opportunities for students from high-poverty, high-minority communities, their strategy might call for reassigning the most experienced and successful principals to low performing schools, adopting a common literacy program

37

for all elementary grades, and creating specialized roles for teacher leaders to serve as instructional coaches. In another district, where central administrators seek to shift more responsibility for improving instruction from the central office to the schools, their strategy might include granting principals the right to decide what mix of instructional and student support positions would be right for their school, setting districtwide criteria for school-based textbook selection, and prescribing an accelerated timetable for hiring teachers. Each of these strategies implies a different approach to managing the relationship between the central office and the schools.

Ideally, our research would have led us to discover a surefire strategy that central office administrators in any district could use to provide the best possible education for all students in all schools. However, identifying one effective strategy is an elusive and likely unrealistic goal. As these brief examples suggest, no single strategy is right for all settings and all circumstances. This doesn't mean, though, that any strategy will do. A workable strategy is neither haphazard nor unfocused. District leaders must purposefully devise a strategy that is responsive to their environment and grounded in a well-informed prediction (often called a *theory of change*) about how that strategy will achieve its goals—"if we do x, then we will accomplish y."

We found that a successful strategy not only is guided by a sensible, realistic theory of change, but it also includes actions and activities that are coherent and mutually reinforcing. Although creating and implementing an effective strategy is admittedly a tall order—especially given the size and complexity of these school districts—that is precisely the challenge that the leaders of the five large urban districts we studied had undertaken.

In this chapter we examine the strategies that these districts adopted for achieving consistent improvement across schools. We focus on three key sets of decisions that reportedly had the greatest effect on teaching and learning in classrooms. These included decisions about the academic program (curriculum, pedagogy, and assessment), budgeting, and staffing. Together, we call these the *strategic priorities* of the central office–schools relationship. Through our in-depth interviews with central office and school leaders, we learned a great deal about how each district devised and implemented its strategy as well as how, and how well, that strategy played out for those in the schools. Although we present no surefire strategy, we do offer important lessons and recommendations for those who take on the challenge of effectively managing a large, complex school system.

WHAT DOES HISTORY TELL US?

For more than two centuries of public education in the United States, reformers typically have touted one of two approaches to district management that stand at opposite ends of a continuum of predictions about how best to manage schools within a district.

At one end of the continuum is *rigorous centralization*, believed by its advocates to improve schooling by concentrating decision-making authority and resources in the central office. At the other end of the continuum is *radical decentralization*, which is said to improve schooling by dispersing decision rights and resources to those in the schools. Centralization and decentralization embody contrasting predictions about the most productive working arrangement between the central office and the schools.

Early in the twentieth century, Frederick Taylor's views on scientific management in industry so impressed influential school reformers that they sought to apply its principles to large, urban districts, creating what historian David Tyack called "the one best system."[1] These reformers believed that by centralizing authority and standardizing best practices, they could improve education for all students. Ellwood P. Cubberly's forecast in 1916 was enthusiastic: "In time it will be possible for any school system to maintain a continuous survey of all the different phases of its work, through tests made by its corps of efficiency experts, and to detect weak points in its work almost as soon as they appear."[2] Despite hopes that a centrally informed and regulated school system would promote expertise and eliminate politics from public education, Tyack found that the values of this model—"efficiency, rationality, continuity, precision and impartiality"—led school officials to ignore the diverse views of constituents and reject their dissent.[3] This approach, which required and rewarded consistency, did yield a measure of order and efficiency to school districts, but it also introduced rigid expectations about curriculum, instruction, and the use of resources that made it hard for schools to tailor programs and practices to meet the needs of their students and local communities.

In the 1990s, proponents of decentralization grounded their reforms in a different set of beliefs. They predicted that transferring resources and decision-making authority from the central office to the schools would eliminate undue restrictions imposed by the district office and liberate schools so that they could respond to the needs and potential of their local school communities. Proponents of school-based management and radical decentralization held to such beliefs.[4]

Yet, again, this theory of change did not produce the benefits its proponents predicted. As education scholar Jerome T. Murphy presciently stated in 1989, "Successful decentralization depends on strong centralization in certain aspects of the organization."[5] For although decentralization gave many schools the flexibility they sought, it also often led to inefficient use of resources and duplication of services across the district. Further, decentralizing control and relying on semiautonomous schools frequently meant that no one closely monitored the level of support and services that different groups of students and communities received. The "haves" tended to get more while the "have-nots" got less. Even when resources were distributed evenly across schools in high-income and low-income neighborhoods, no one could say for sure that the social and instructional needs of students from all communities were being fairly and successfully met, because schools in low-income communities often needed more per-pupil resources to educate their students. Equal distribution of funds and services to autonomous or semiautonomous schools did not necessarily lead to equity.

Neither approach reliably led to successful outcomes for all students. School administrators who were committed to ensuring effective instruction for all students in all classrooms could not count on simple beliefs about the value of uniform or differentiated practices for school governance. Over time, reformers began to recognize that effectively managing a system of schools requires a complex strategy that at once ensures high standards, support, and opportunity for all students in all schools while promoting the innovation, investment, and commitment that principals, teachers, and local school communities can provide. Over the past decade, many school officials have tried to find the right balance between centralized regulation and school-site discretion as they developed their strategy for managing schools.

NO SINGLE STRATEGY

All of the districts we studied adopted distinctive strategies that included some mix of centralized and decentralized approaches to manage their academic program, staffing, and budgeting. However, we did see patterns across the five districts in the theory of change that grounded their local strategy. Broadly, the districts fell at different points on the continuum of beliefs running from centralization to decentralization (see figure 2.1).

FIGURE 2.1   Centralization-Decentralization continuum for five districts

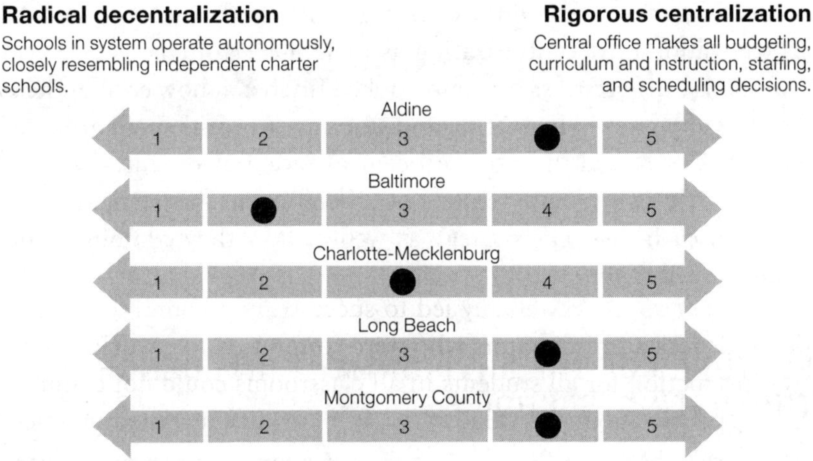

Radical decentralization
Schools in system operate autonomously, closely resembling independent charter schools.

Rigorous centralization
Central office makes all budgeting, curriculum and instruction, staffing, and scheduling decisions.

Three districts (Aldine, Long Beach, and Montgomery County) tended to rely on centralized and standardized policies and practices, which they predicted would improve learning districtwide. Two others (Baltimore and Charlotte-Mecklenburg) adhered to a very different theory of change, predicting that decentralized control and differentiated practices would lead to better instruction in their schools.

Having a sound, realistic theory of change is essential so that everyone understands how a set of strategic activities can be expected to move the district forward toward achieving an important goal. However, based on our research in these five districts, we concluded that a good theory of change was not enough. What mattered more was whether the parts of that strategy worked together coherently to support the work of teachers and administrators at the school and in classrooms. In other words, either centralized or decentralized approaches can be successful. Ultimately, achieving coherence depended much more on how a strategy was developed and implemented than on the general theory of change that guided it.

Nonetheless, the continuum of centralization and decentralization provides a useful starting point for our analysis. We looked first at how these five districts handled key decisions about their academic program—what curriculum teachers would use, how it would be taught, and how students' learning would be assessed. Although we found similarities among the subset of districts that relied on either centralization or decentralization as their theory of change, we also saw notable differences. When we looked further at how each of these districts approached budgeting and staffing, the same small group of districts had placed their bets on centralization or decentralization. However, we again found important differences in the particular elements of each district's strategy as well as how they combined and implemented them.

FEATURES OF THE ENVIRONMENT INFLUENCE THE DISTRICTS' CHOICES

No district chooses a theory of change or adopts a strategy in a vacuum. Inevitably, features of the district's external environment shape what is possible and what happens with any set of strategic activities. For example, since 2000, levels of centralization and standardization have increased across virtually all U.S. school districts due to new federal and state policies. No Child Left Behind combined with the states' expansion of standardized testing and the financial incentives embedded in Race to the Top have led many district officials to require that schools follow more consistent practices. Despite this broad push toward standardization, some district officials have decided to grant more autonomy to schools, yet in doing so they cannot disregard state or federal policies. Therefore, in understanding the decisions that district administrators make, it's important to see how the environment of the school system affects the options that district leaders have and the choices they make.

For example, when Charlotte-Mecklenburg's school board hired Peter Gorman in 2006, it gave him a mandate to relax the strict control of curriculum and instruction that his predecessors in the central office had imposed. At the same time, North Carolina's education regulations limited the discretion that principals could exercise in hiring and assigning teachers. Thus, Gorman had to find a way to meet his board's expectations for freeing schools within the constraints of laws that limited principals' discretion.

Wanda Bamberg had been superintendent for more than three years when we visited Aldine. She was committed to maintaining consistent practices across the Aldine schools. In pursuing a strategy that was based on beliefs about the benefits of centralization, she benefited not only from her long tenure as an employee in the district but also from the school district's stable history and traditions of centralized local school governance, which were further bolstered by Texas's sustained, high-profile emphasis on standardized testing.

Therefore, any district's strategy for managing district-schools relationships was influenced not only by its predictions about the benefits of centralization or decentralization but also by an array of environmental factors, such as the history of the district, state laws and regulations, and economic realities. Of course, all of this makes the work of devising and implementing a coherent strategy for instructional improvement complex and daunting.

A CLOSE LOOK AT STRATEGIES

We take a close look at the strategies used by these five districts to manage their academic program (curriculum, pedagogy, and assessment). Three districts—Aldine, Long Beach, and Montgomery County—chose centralization as their theory of change. Each, however, adopted and implemented a distinctive strategy (see figure 2.2).

Similarly, in examining Baltimore and Charlotte-Mecklenburg, we found that both districts relied on predictions about the benefits of decentralization yet chose different elements for their strategy and experienced different levels of success in implementing it.

Three Districts' Centralized Approaches

When we visited Aldine, Long Beach, and Montgomery County, we found that for some years each district had relied on a centralized approach to managing the relationship between the district office and the schools. Recent changes in the environment—especially increased demands for accountability, as well as funding crises caused by the economic recession—had further reinforced those

FIGURE 2.2   Where are academic programming decisions made?

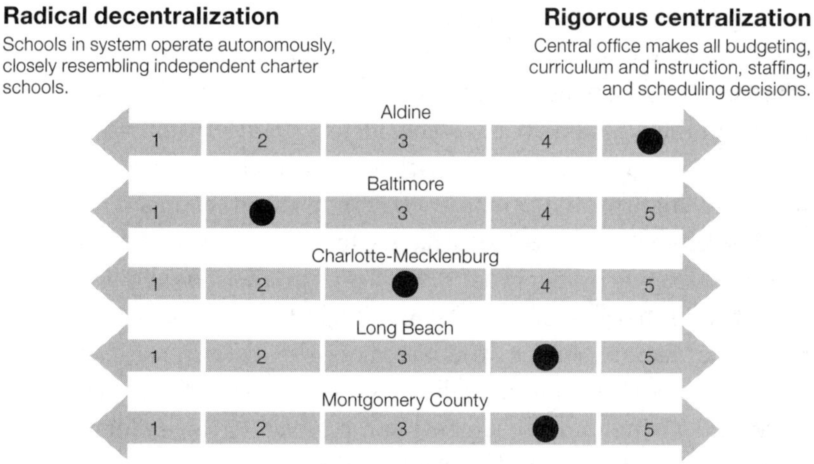

Radical decentralization
Schools in system operate autonomously, closely resembling independent charter schools.

Rigorous centralization
Central office makes all budgeting, curriculum and instruction, staffing, and scheduling decisions.

leanings. These three districts adhered to a similar "If-then" prediction as they designed their academic program: *if the district can use its resources and expertise to adopt or develop high-quality curriculum, provide excellent professional development, and monitor the curriculum's implementation with assessments, then all teachers will be supported in instruction and all students will learn.*

Aldine—Managing for Instructional Uniformity. Of the five districts, Aldine's strategy for managing its academic program relied most on centralization. The district office established the most standardized practices, expecting schools to closely follow its mandated curriculum and assessments. It required teachers to use a prescribed pedagogy—"managed instruction." District officials provided sample lessons and laid out what teachers were to cover every six weeks. Superintendent Bamberg explained that school board policy defined this process: "The idea is, we're going to let you [the teacher] know what to teach and when. We're going to tell you and work with you on the best ways to teach it and we're going to have an assessment of [whether what you do] is aligned to what we've provided for you." This strategy to achieve instructional regularity across all classrooms was in line with Texas's aggressive accountability policies and standardized tests.

Bamberg described Aldine's efforts to establish common practices across all schools and classes: "We say, 'We're going to do these district tests and we're going to do these lessons.' And when we have an issue with a curriculum, we get very prescriptive . . . We say, 'Here's Monday's lesson. Here's Tuesday.'" Bamberg made it clear that district officials were not reluctant to exercise authority: "You're going to teach algebra this way."

Bamberg said that Aldine's pursuit of academic quality and consistency called for "constant training" of teachers and ongoing supervision of principals. When district officials identified schools for intervention, she explained, they "truly expect the principal to lead the way . . . The principal has to do it. So ultimately we tell the principal, 'You're responsible for making sure this instruction happens the way it's supposed to, when it's supposed to.'"

Although principals were expected to see that teachers complied with the district's requirements, they did not see their role in the process as heavy-handed. For example, one high school principal talked about the "bottom line" in the teachers' instructional planning meetings: "If there is input [that the principals] need to give, then it's given. However, we'll build a relationship with the teachers such that they don't see our input as threatening. It's not a mandate." An elementary school principal similarly described both the far reach of Aldine's instructional prescriptions and his tolerance for variation: "My teachers know that you're held accountable for teaching standards, curriculum, and standards. We know what works for kids. Your research-based instructional strategies [work]. Now, how and when you do it, that's up to those teachers. You can walk from one classroom to another classroom and they're not doing it the same way. They're being in their own style and their own personality, but they're having success."

Long Beach—A Consistent Academic Program Adapted by the Schools. Long Beach's strategy to achieve overall consistency in its academic program originated years before, when the district adopted the Open Court literacy program. The deputy superintendent explained that Open Court "provided a foundation that every teacher could use" to achieve a basic level of success, "and then we were able to build on that and our excellent teachers were able to go beyond." Superintendent Steinhauser concurred: "Teachers were trained in certain basics . . . [but] people were given the flexibility to take it to the next level, based on data and performance."

Long Beach had common textbook adoptions, a pacing schedule for all grades and subjects, common quarterly and end-of-course exams, and common instructional strategies. High schools used the same course outlines and academic vocabulary. Despite this level of standardization, the deputy superintendent emphasized the "loose" elements of their tight-loose approach to managing the academic program: "Now, there is still flexibility within that. The nonnegotiables are the key assignments, the assessment, pacing within the [prescribed] range. But if they can justify to the principal why they've accelerated or slowed down, that [adjustment] is okay. They know when they have to get to a certain point for the assessment, so we trust our teachers with that."

Schools implemented the required course pathways in various ways. Steinhauser estimated that there were five or six engineering pathways at different high schools, each allowing for a different sequence of courses. "So it's just the differentiation of how we deliver the content, but the content and what the kids have to demonstrate in terms of their knowledge is the same." An assistant superintendent illustrated how this variation played out:

> Our course outlines are consistent all the way through. So, if you're English I, II [at the high school level] the course outline is the same across the district—across the schools, across the academies. What makes yours different is your delivery of the content. So if the standard is to teach the historical context of *To Kill a Mockingbird* in the arts academy, I might do that through pictures of the Dust Bowl and experiences with Billie Holiday's "Strange Fruit." If I'm in a business academy, it might be more in-depth study of the stock market crash to set the historical context. If I'm in a social justice academy, it might be a real deep study of the Jim Crow laws and some of the legislation at the time.

Most Long Beach teachers also used a common approach to lessons inspired by Madeline Hunter, whose instructional model was widely adopted during the 1970s and 1980s. One Long Beach administrator explained that their local approach to pedagogy had been "built over time and retooled and refreshed." Through professional development, teachers were "taught different ways to use that structure," some "more deductive" and others "more inductive." While acknowledging that there was "definitely standardization" in the curriculum resources available to teachers, she expressed confidence that "teachers would also tell you that they've had a lot of access to supplemental resources and to having a say in adding a layer on top of the standard curriculum." Principals widely confirmed both the required components of the academic program and the flexibility that the district's strategy gave them to adapt it to different types of schools, pathways, and students.

Montgomery County—A Locally Developed Curriculum Used Districtwide. Whereas Aldine and Long Beach relied substantially on prepared curricula and outside experts to build their academic program, Montgomery County had a centralized Office of Curriculum and Instructional Programs, where staff developed most of the district's curriculum and course materials. When we visited, the district was producing a major upgrade of its curriculum—Curriculum 2.0—designed to align with the new Common Core State Standards and to provide an online system for teachers' curriculum, lesson planning, and professional development. A high school principal said that he was "blown away by how incredible [Curriculum 2.0] is and also how a teacher can enhance it, how a teacher can differentiate it, so it's not just a curriculum anymore."

Regular student assessments were key to the district's overall strategy. Some years earlier, Montgomery County had set the goal of having 80 percent of their students graduate "college-ready" by 2014.[6] With that in mind, curriculum planners mapped the district's curriculum clear back to kindergarten, setting benchmark targets for seven transition points, including third grade reading proficiency and success in eighth grade algebra. They also created a "monitoring calendar" that district administrators used with each principal to review his or her school's performance. The curriculum did not include pacing guides, although the assessments eventually showed whether teachers had adhered to the curricula. One administrator explained, "You've got to lay the groundwork. This is our curriculum. You have to assess these kids. You have to look at the data. We're going to be checking it. I think you have to do that."

When we visited Montgomery County, Josh Starr had recently been appointed superintendent and was taking stock of the district's approach to assessment. He was concerned that their intense focus on student achievement data might lead teachers to unduly focus time and attention on certain students—those "on the bubble" whose improved test scores could make the school's standing rise under

NCLB: "You need people who understand the school improvement process, who can coach, who can think through what it is they want kids to know and be able to do and what teachers have to do around that. It's the opposite of the AYP 'bubble' focus."

Principals still said that they monitored whether teachers followed the curriculum. When asked how much flexibility she had in implementing the curriculum, one middle school principal answered equivocally, "a lot and none, quite honestly." There were important choices to be made, but the boundaries in which they could be made were well-defined. She was pleased that "the curriculum comes to us . . . Our teachers aren't out writing curriculum . . . [There is] a huge OSP office to provide supports." She relied on the district's specialists in each content area and said that she could always get district administrators' attention when she had ideas or concerns about curriculum. An elementary school principal said that he appreciated the gradual rollout of Curriculum 2.0, which provided both constraints and choices, allowing him and his teachers to "make it our own."

Do Educators at All Levels of the System Inform Centralized Practices?

Across these three districts, we learned that policies and practices succeeded when they were continuously informed by the knowledge, skills, and experience of educators from all levels of the system. A centralized policy stood a better chance of being supported by those in the schools if teachers and principals had played at least an advisory role in its development and regularly reviewed it. For example, Montgomery County teachers participated in reviewing textbook selection and advised the district administrators responsible for developing curriculum. Long Beach relied on pilot projects to gather feedback and explore the quality and effectiveness of initiatives before extending them to all schools. Once the district tested and adjusted a policy or program, it was "rolled out" to all schools, and many who had been involved in its creation and piloting voiced confidence in the reforms they advanced.

Experience from Aldine suggests that receiving feedback from teachers and principals can be contentious, no matter how correct or informative central office administrators think it is. Superintendent Bamberg told of asking math specialists and principals who had been math teachers to offer feedback about benchmark assessments in mathematics. She told teachers that they would have the chance to give feedback on the assessments for one year only: "'We're going to take your feedback after every series of tests this year . . . And then the committee that writes the test will look at your feedback and they will decide whether or not they will make the changes.' I said, 'Quite frankly, I don't want to hear any more about it after this year.'" Further, she rejected complaints brought by a group of teachers about a set of items that long had been included in the fourth grade test. In response to their criticisms, she said, "Well that's good. I'm glad to hear that. But apparently if you've been sending that information in and you've written it down and you've sent it to the committee, apparently the committee doesn't agree with you . . . That's the committee's decision."

Reciprocal exchanges between those in the schools and those in the central office proved to be difficult in Aldine when administrators and teachers at the two levels disagreed about where academic expertise resides and who should have the final say. Introducing and adapting curricula in Long Beach and Montgomery County was never a one-time event but a continuous process that required training and refinement as both teachers and administrators gained experience and knowledge using the curriculum. Over time it led to greater trust among school-based and central office officials. A district's strategy was only as good as the central administrators' judgment and ongoing interest in gaining more feedback and providing support. When they truly relied on school-based educators' experience and advice, trust grew within schools about the good intentions of central administrators. However, trust could quickly disappear if teachers and principals saw the district's request for feedback as no more than a symbolic nod to participation. Achieving the district's mission of effectively educating all students necessarily rested on widespread confidence that everyone involved was committed to learning more and getting better at what they did. This continuous, systemic improvement was fueled and steadied by the mutual respect established through day-to-day work interactions among those at all levels of the system.

Two Districts' Decentralized Academic Programs

In Charlotte-Mecklenburg and Baltimore, central office administrators were in the process of decentralizing district-schools relationships by granting schools more flexibility and discretion in decision making. Although district leaders had similar beliefs about the benefits of decentralization, they differed in one key element of their strategy: when and under what circumstances schools should be granted autonomy. Charlotte-Mecklenburg granted flexibility to schools as a reward for successful performance, while Baltimore granted autonomy as a precondition for improvement. This fundamental difference in the two districts' approaches played out in how they implemented seemingly similar strategies for improving the academic program.

Charlotte-Mecklenburg—The Pendulum Swings Back. Before Peter Gorman became Charlotte-Mecklenburg's superintendent, the district relied on a highly prescriptive pedagogical strategy called "managed instruction." Gorman's predecessor, reportedly dismayed by the use of forty-one different reading programs across the district, required that only one, Open Court, be used. The district imposed a tight timetable for assessing students' progress. The chief academic officer (CAO) recalled: "We had a ten-page document of nonnegotiables, a very tightly scripted process across all content areas."

Critics of earlier administrators' demands for standardization wanted more discretion in what was taught and how it was taught. Once Gorman became superintendent, the pendulum started to swing back toward decentralization. He still required that Open Court be used, but it was one of only three nonnegotiables—the others being "follow the law" and "teach North Carolina's standard course of study." Gorman permitted and encouraged variation in the rest of the curriculum from school to school. Under Freedom and Flexibility, he granted more school-site autonomy to principals whose students achieved high scores on standardized tests. Although Freedom and Flexibility was earned, at the time of our visit it seemed not to be highly selective, because 115 of 178 of the principals had gained the privilege. Other principals were said to choose their own programs by, as one said, "flying under the radar," which reportedly worked well when test scores were high. However, in the current context of accountability, variation in what was taught flourished far less than one might expect in a district that was banking on decentralization. This was true even in the 115 schools that had earned considerable discretion, in part because the district assessed students across all schools on the same topics at the same time of year, leading teachers to conform to the recommended topics and timetable. Schools that received the most prescription and oversight by central office administrators were either receiving Title I funding or performing poorly on standardized tests, or both.

Still, principals described a substantial swing toward school-site management under Gorman's leadership. One elementary school principal said that four or five years earlier teachers heard the following message from administrators: "Hey, you'd better be on page such-and-such of the pacing guide when we come into your classroom." In 2012 he characterized the message very differently: "You know, that curriculum, in and of itself, with our population, isn't rigorous enough. We've got to do more. We've got to push. We've got to enrich. We've got to move forward." He thought that students benefited when the schools and teachers had more autonomy to teach as they thought best. "That is one of the things I think has really changed for the better with our current leadership—that [for schools that show] they know what they're doing, there is definitely a push toward doing more rigorous instruction and more relevant things."

Administrators said that having more discretion at the school site depended on maintaining high performance. When schools fell back, central office administrators returned to closer oversight, confronting principals with evidence of the problems they saw. The CAO said that a central administrator supervising the principal of such a school might say, "Okay, here's what we're seeing. We've made this huge investment in [the curriculum] Math Forward. These are the kinds of results we're seeing when it's implemented with fidelity. Here are the places

where we don't see the fidelity of implementation [in your school]."
She explained, "It's not a 'gotcha.' It's just . . . how we apply pressure and support." Although we found some evidence that the central office was reclaiming its right to regulate school-level academic
practices, those moves seemed to involve more coaxing than com-
manding. Routine supervisory practices in Charlotte-Mecklenburg
differed from those in Aldine, Long Beach, or Montgomery County,
where district officials routinely reviewed student achievement data
with principals and expected compliance with many district policies
and practices.

Baltimore—Autonomy Bounded with Guidance. Andrés Alonso,
who had been CEO in Baltimore for five years, believed that those
closest to instruction—the teachers, principals, and parents—knew
better than central officials about how to improve the schools. Therefore, he wanted schools and teachers to exercise more control and
not be obliged to comply automatically with directives from district
officials. He believed that "the action" was in the schools, not in the
central office, and that those who interacted most directly with students and the school community should take the lead in setting their
school's academic program, building its budget, and hiring its staff.
Therefore, a key element of Baltimore's strategy was that schools
should have autonomy from the start, not as a reward for successful
performance.

In their interviews, many principals recalled the illogical and
arbitrary dictates from the central office under prior administrations.
One told about how his school had achieved great progress in literacy
only to be told by a central administrator to adopt a new reading program just three days before school started: "I—in the language of a
teenage girl—threw a hissy fit. 'No, I'm not going to do this.'" With
full backing from his teachers, the principal successfully sought and
won charter status for his school.

On arrival, Alonso decided that students were paying a price
when the district imposed unwarranted requirements on the schools.
He drastically cut the size of the central office and pushed authority
for making decisions about the academic program, budgeting, and

staffing to the schools—*all* schools, not just those that had demonstrated success. Delegating control to the schools did not achieve immediate success. At first, schools varied widely in the academic programs they adopted and the progress they made. Many principals were used to being told what to do and complying with the requirements imposed by the central office. Several recalled that when Alonso gave them both autonomy and responsibility for improving their schools, they needed more skills than they had and more assistance than they received.

Alonso responded to this unevenness in school-site capacity and outcomes by encouraging—but not mandating—more consistency. This was especially apparent in his response to new academic standards that would be used across most states in assessing accountability: "The Common Core is not going to be about schools defining what the standards are. So, I felt [that] where we had loosened the conversation about school practice, that I now needed . . . to tighten the conversation about standards." He wanted his central office to provide support for making the "transition to a different definition of what kids need to be able to do."

The newly appointed CAO, an expert in literacy, issued specific "guidance" about the kind of instruction that schools should provide. She observed that the Common Core "just came at a really good time. And if it hadn't been the Common Core, we would have needed the shift anyway." At the time of our interviews, her office was developing a set of "fundamentals" that all schools would be expected to address. She explained that these addressed such things as "what a ninety-minute literacy block needs to look like" or "how time should be used in a seventh-grade or middle-grades math class. These are the components that should be part of a high school ELA period or math period, or an algebra II class." Principals widely respected her expertise and found her approach helpful, not needlessly restrictive. As one said, it "still allows us to staff and create the programs for the children."

As Baltimore's strategy evolved, "guidance" from the central office came coupled with training. Central office staff supported the schools' newfound curricular autonomy with assistance, but only some program options came with professional development. Schools could choose curricula that the district did not support— assuming they met certain criteria—but schools would have to pay for the program's products and training. As a result, most schools chose the options supported by the district. The CAO explained that she and others in the central office introduced a new assessment system to monitor progress. The "non-negotiable is that you must properly monitor students' reading, K through 3. That's the nonnegotiable because that's best practice." She reported that "some schools opted for their own [program], which is fine. But literally 90 percent of our elementary schools use the one assessment, because we sold them on it first." She reflected on the schools' decisions: "If we make people smarter, they'll make better choices."

Baltimore's central administrators initially worried that schools might head in many different directions—some promising, others not. However, they found that having options drew principals and teachers into productive discussions about the fundamentals of instruction. One district administrator said that questions surfaced, such as, "'How do we teach a guided reading lesson?' or 'How do we teach seventh grade math?'" These, he explained, are "questions that I think school leaders and their teams need to grapple with. I would hope that it makes them smarter, more self-assured, and more willing to make an informed decision." A high school principal confirmed this view, saying that the CAO had "brought real academic focus back to the district." Just as the Common Core standards had provided the CAO with a convincing rationale for expecting more of principals and teachers, this principal thought the CAO's new academic focus gave him "the momentum he needed to say to his staff: 'Okay, we're great, but we're not great enough to start going where she's talking about going.' And so, you know, my team was willing to pick up on that, too."

Decentralization played out differently in the schools of Charlotte-Mecklenburg and Baltimore. The prospect of gaining greater autonomy was used as an incentive for better performance in Charlotte-Mecklenburg. Once gained, central administrators expected this earned autonomy to spur on schools to explore and adopt different academic approaches. We never learned whether earned autonomy led to more exploration, but principals who had been granted Freedom and Flexibility endorsed the approach. We did hear that schools often seized and exercised autonomy, even if the central office had not granted it, leading to an academic program that differed from school to school, possibly in response to local needs and opportunities.

In contrast, central administrators in Baltimore granted schools autonomy to choose their academic program, expecting that it would lead principals and teachers to make sound decisions based on their students' needs. Paradoxically, as school leaders there experienced new freedom and anticipated the Common Core standards, they increasingly relied on skilled and trusted central administrators for training and support, which in turn led to a more consistent academic program across the district.

Do Sufficient Knowledge and Expertise Exist in the Central Office and the Schools?

A district that delegates decisions and resources to its schools has to count on having informed expertise among the teachers and principals, who then choose curricula, teach or supervise instruction, and assess student progress. One lesson that CEO Alonso learned most quickly when he granted more autonomy to the schools was that principals needed help as they stepped up to their new responsibilities. It was not only that they might make poor choices without the benefit of expert advice but also that they often lacked skills in such things as literacy instruction or data analysis. Only with support from more skilled and knowledgeable educators in the system could all principals effectively exercise their newfound autonomy. Because principals respected the CAO's expertise in literacy, they could confidently choose curricula and professional development, with her guidance.

Also, those in the schools needed to be able to count on district officials to help them get things done throughout the system. As in many large urban districts, Baltimore principals were used to responding to orders from central administrators who had authority over functions such as assessment, budgeting, or staffing. The introduction of bounded autonomy encouraged them to be creative and develop practices that were responsive to the needs of their students and local community. Still, even the most determined and informed principals were sometimes deterred by deeply rooted, bureaucratic procedures. Recognizing this problem, the superintendent created intermediary network teams, including specialists in areas such as student support, academics, or special education. These specialists not only could provide advice, but they also could troubleshoot problems that principals encountered with the bureaucracy. Principals appreciated the help but noted that some specialists were more effective than others. Baltimore's experience illustrates both the importance and the challenge of ensuring that expertise runs throughout the system and is readily available to those at all levels who make decisions and provide services.

DID DISTRICTS HAVE SIMILAR STRATEGIES FOR THE ACADEMIC PROGRAM, BUDGETING, AND STAFFING?

As we have seen, three districts relied on a theory of change grounded in beliefs about the promise of centralization, while two others instituted strategies that were guided by the potential they saw in decentralization. We wondered whether districts that pursued notably centralized or decentralized approaches in defining their academic program also did so for the other key strategic priorities, budgeting and staffing. That is, did Aldine manage its academic program, budgeting, and staffing from the central office? And did Baltimore promote school-site autonomy with guidance in all three strategic priorities? The general answer to these questions is yes, but there were notable differences, suggesting that these priorities were associated but not tightly bound together.

Budgeting

We found consistent patterns in how the districts funded their schools. Aldine, Long Beach, and Montgomery County—those that defined and regulated their academic program centrally—allocated funds using a per-pupil formula. This strategy was intended to ensure that all schools would be dealt with in an even-handed way based on student enrollments. In contrast, Baltimore and Charlotte-Mecklenburg, which allowed schools substantial autonomy to manage their academic program, gave schools larger sums to serve students with greater needs. (See figure 2.3 for a continuum of where budgeting decisions were made in the five districts.)

This differentiated allocation strategy, called "fair student funding" in Baltimore and "weighted student funding" in Charlotte-Mecklenburg, allowed some local schools more resources than others to meet their students' particular needs. This element of their strategy aligned well with their readiness to have schools adopt different academic programs in response to local needs. Superintendent Gorman reported that, as a result of weighted student funding, Charlotte-Mecklenburg funded one particular elementary school at $4,200 per pupil, which made it possible to fund another school at $10,200 per pupil: "For every kid [at the first school], we're grabbing $3,000 and shipping it to [the second school]." Gorman said that this policy had achieved the results they sought: "We've gotten the increases

FIGURE 2.3   Where are budgeting decisions made?

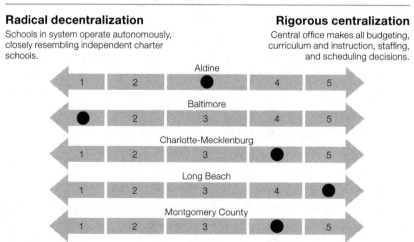

in graduation rate, the closing of the achievement gap. We've done it through differentiated resource allocation."

However, other aspects of budgeting deviated somewhat from these two policies of per-pupil and weighted student funding, illustrating the variations in strategies used across our sample. For example, all five districts received extra federal Title I funding for schools that enrolled students from low-income families. Given that these districts served many such students, revenue from Title I and its state equivalent was sizeable. Aldine's Bamberg said that $20 million in Title I funds allowed eligible campuses to hire extra staff or launch new programs. After the central office had taken "some off the top" to support administration, the schools had "full flexibility" to spend those funds. Long Beach, another district favoring centralized approaches, responded very differently in coping with cuts in external funding. Administrators there consolidated all Title I funds in the central office and used them to support districtwide programs and services that otherwise would go unfunded. The Long Beach principals we interviewed who had once counted on Title I funds to support key initiatives regretted their loss but acknowledged the district's effort to maintain its priorities.

Meanwhile, Charlotte-Mecklenburg, which granted many schools autonomy in choosing curriculum, restricted how principals could use Title I funds and required central district approval of their decisions. A principal who was accustomed to having more discretion in making decisions about her school said that she found the controls "restrictive." She explained, "I need to be able to do whatever I need to do, since I'm going to be held accountable for those results." In one of the district's academic zones, which included only Title I–eligible schools, the district pooled Title I money to serve general needs across those schools. As the zone superintendent explained, this allowed district officials to "use those dollars a little bit more strategically, such as buying the math program" for all schools in the zone. Thus, Charlotte-Mecklenburg, a district that promoted autonomy in curriculum and funded schools using a weighted student formula, responded to financial cuts at the state level by taking centralized control of Title I funds, which once had been the principals' to allocate.

Staffing

Staffing practices, too, conformed to these broader patterns of centralization and decentralization (see figure 2.4).

District staff screened and recruited candidates in Aldine, Long Beach, and Montgomery County, while principals in Baltimore and Charlotte-Mecklenburg had much more responsibility for those activities. This made sense, since a centralized approach to the academic program permitted the district office to project and meet the staffing needs across all local schools. Conversely, if a district granted autonomy to the school for its academic program, a principal would expect to hire teachers to match the school's needs and choices. Notably, principals in all districts retained at least some control over new hires, reflecting a current belief in public education that school leaders should have the final say about who teaches in their school.

Aldine and Montgomery County recruited teaching candidates nationally and internationally, screened them, and then permitted principals to interview prospective teachers and decide whom to hire. Principals were not allowed to hire candidates who came to

FIGURE 2.4   Where are staffing decisions made?

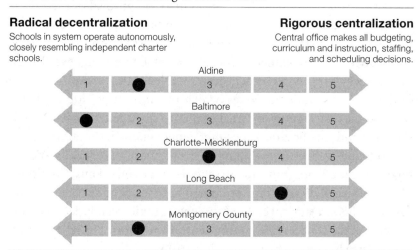

them directly without prescreening by the district. In Aldine, a court decree required principals to abide by racial and ethnic guidelines in hiring teachers. In both districts, principals generally endorsed the in-school services provided by the district's human resource specialists and praised the depth of the candidate pool that the district recruited. Long Beach had a similar hiring process, although the job offer eventually was made by the central office rather than the principal who supported the decision and would supervise the new teacher. At the time we visited, Montgomery County was experimenting with an expanded screening process for all teaching candidates in the district, which required them to complete a writing assignment that was then reviewed centrally by a small, trained group of teachers and principals. Such an approach would set a high bar for new teachers' writing skills across all schools, but by having school-level personnel assess the writing, they could ensure that the expectations would be informed and appropriate.

In contrast, Baltimore and Charlotte-Mecklenburg relied more on principals to seek out, review, and hire candidates. This approach ideally allowed them to match their programmatic and staffing needs. However, tenure guarantees and transfer policies often restricted the principal's right to decide who would teach in his or her school. Baltimore's district office had long hired and then assigned teachers to schools in a decidedly top-down way. However, under Alonso, principals were doing much more interviewing. One said, "It's not just the district saying, 'I've got a teacher. I've got a spot. Put them together.'" Another explained, "I kind of seek out and recruit my own teachers, because I know what I'm looking for." However, before principals could offer jobs to candidates, they had to satisfy administrators in the Office of Human Capital that the applicant was "highly qualified" under NCLB.

School site administrators in Charlotte-Mecklenburg could exercise considerable discretion in interviewing candidates. One principal explained that once he posts a position, "Downtown gives us viable candidates and I have an interview committee, which teachers volunteer for . . . We interview all the candidates who are sent to us. I share the resumes I have. We have a three- or four-page document with questions that cover everything from classroom management to curriculum, working on a team, what they see as their future, how they work outside the box." Some Charlotte-Mecklenburg principals also said that in an effort to meet their school's staffing needs, they identified candidates on their own, asking them to apply, and then shepherding them through the screening process at the central office. However, Charlotte-Mecklenburg's process was more centralized than one might expect, given its shift toward greater school-site autonomy. In part, this resulted from the district's need to find assignments for all tenured teachers who had been displaced from their positions due to program cuts, a challenge that all districts experienced.

Therefore, in both budgeting and staffing, the districts' practices were, for the most part, similar to those they had adopted for their academic program. Central office administrators in Aldine, Long Beach, and Montgomery retained more responsibility and control over each of these strategic priorities than did their counterparts in Charlotte-Mecklenburg and Baltimore. However, these districts did not adopt uniform, lock-step responses in all three areas. We saw evidence of this in Aldine's policy of allowing schools to spend their Title I funds, as well as Charlotte-Mecklenburg's reliance on the district office for recruiting, screening, and distributing candidates.

SUMMARY

As these accounts suggest, we found that different theories of change guided these five districts' strategies for managing relationships with their schools. Three were committed to centralized approaches, and two favored decentralized approaches. In Aldine, Long Beach, and Montgomery County, central office administrators retained considerable control over curriculum, pedagogy, and assessment, although these district leaders conceived of their responsibilities somewhat differently across the three districts. One important factor that contributed to successful implementation was whether those in the schools continued to inform, review, and recommend revisions in the decisions that central administrators made. When district- and school-level educators worked in a reciprocal relationship, with teachers and principals having a meaningful say in centralized policies and practices, we found greater acceptance of and respect for the district's role, and there was greater coherence across its policies and practices.

By contrast, in Baltimore and Charlotte-Mecklenburg—both of which had been under tight, centralized control prior to the current superintendent's administration—schools exercised more autonomy in decisions about curriculum, budgeting, and staffing. Although principals generally welcomed the flexibility they were granted— either as a reward for improvement, as in Charlotte-Mecklenburg, or as a precondition of improvement, as in Baltimore—principals did not always have the skills and knowledge they needed to carry out their expanded responsibilities. This became especially clear in Baltimore, where Alonso's strategy of bounded autonomy could only succeed if both central and school administrators had deep knowledge and strong skills. Short of that, they had to acquire what they lacked through training and support. It might seem self-evident that a district should hire and develop skilled and knowledgeable educators at all levels of the system; however, the importance of this requirement became starkly apparent in once-centralized Baltimore when Alonso chose a strategy for improvement that rested on delegating responsibility and resources to those in the schools.

LESSONS FOR PRACTICE

We chose these five districts because each had a record of improvement and success. From them we learned how a district's theory of change and its strategy might ultimately improve student learning throughout the district. This leads us to suggest the following lessons for practice:

⊃ *You need both a theory of change and a strategy to bring about meaningful change.* The districts had different predictions, or theories of change, to guide their approaches to central office–schools relationships. Some believed in the promise of centralization; others placed their bets on decentralization. Although it's important to have a practical theory of change to guide action, that's not enough. You need to pair your theory of change with a clearly conceived strategy, which includes compatible actions and activities that are likely to produce better results.

⊃ *You can choose a centralized theory of action, a decentralized theory of action, or some combination of the two.* A centralized approach may well have strategic actions and activities that encourage or accommodate variation from school to school, just as a decentralized approach may well call for some level of standardization. Purity is not the point; practical coherence is.

⊃ *Remember that trust matters in building productive central office–schools relationships.* Central office administrators may willingly cede authority to principals and teachers (or vice versa) as long as all the players are confident that they will be respected and fairly treated.

⊃ *If you choose programs or practices that are to be implemented districtwide, be sure to engage teachers and principals early and often in reviewing them and suggesting improvements.* Providing structured opportunities for those in the schools to shape and improve standardized practices will increase their effectiveness and enhance the commitment of those responsible for implementing them. This suggests that district leaders need to develop frequent, ongoing opportunities for reciprocal influence between the central office and the schools.

⊃ *If you decide to grant greater autonomy to those in the schools, be sure that principals and teachers have the training and support they need to make good decisions.* This requires developing skills, knowledge, and expertise at all levels of the system. Those in the schools will need time and resources to support their training. Also, district administrators will need to become skilled in providing that training and the ongoing support that follows.

THREE

Achieving Coherence in Practice

The idea that school districts need to achieve coherence in order to perform at high levels may seem obvious. For when the parts of the organization operate in harmony, work gets done, goals are met, people feel satisfied with their jobs, and children learn. Although the need for coherence may seem like common sense, coherent practices often are hard to observe and even more difficult to explain. What does the arrangement of the resources, systems, and structures of a school district look like when they are compatible and coherent? How do academic programming, budgeting, and staffing work when they are mutually reinforcing? In this chapter, we explain and illustrate what coherence means in practice by examining how the organizational elements and strategic priorities operate in the central office–schools relationship for the districts we studied.

In order to understand coherence and to see how it can strengthen implementation of a district's strategy, it is helpful to first look closely at how the resources, structures, and systems—the means by which most work is deliberately accomplished—are arranged and used to achieve goals, large and small. It is these organizational elements that newly appointed leaders most often target for reform. They are the *how* of reform. That is, leaders implement reforms by altering the resources, structures, and systems in the school district. *Resources*, which include not only dollars but also such things as human capital or professionals' time, fund and fuel the district's activities. *Structures* include the array of positions, roles, and responsibilities that individuals hold as they do their work. *Systems* are the various processes and procedures by which that work is carried out. Superintendents' entry plans, school board initiatives, and districts' strategic plans typically burst with promises and proposals to redirect resources (e.g., fund parent outreach), reorganize structures (e.g., create school-site committees), and redesign systems (e.g., coordinate teacher induction across schools). Despite the prominent attention that district officials commit to changes in resource allocation, structures, and systems, those intended reforms often are implemented in patchwork, uncoordinated ways. Too frequently they end up operating separately and sometimes at odds in bureaucratic silos (the finance office, the cabinet, the human resources department).

We found that when the components of the district's organization worked coherently together, they supported and advanced the district's strategy. For example, Aldine coordinated its professional development, accountability systems, and budgetary resources to meet its goal of improving students' performance on the state tests. However, when resources, systems, and structures were incompatible or contradicted one another, the result was an incoherent, poorly implemented strategy. Lacking explicit efforts to create order in their use of resources, systems, and structures, district leaders might struggle unsuccessfully to achieve their goals without understanding why or how their well-intentioned plans went awry.

We also learned that there could be coherence (as well as incoherence) among the three strategic priorities that are central to the relationship between the district and the schools—academic programming, budgeting, and staffing. Whereas the organizational elements are the *how* of reform, the strategic priorities are the *what*. When districts implement changes in resources, systems, and structures to alter the central office–schools relationship, it is the strategic priorities that they are intending to affect. For example, when a central office department is restructured, the goal is to improve some aspect of academic programming, budgeting, and staffing, or how these strategic priorities work together. We found that the strategic priorities had to be mutually compatible and reinforcing if they were to support a district's strategy. When they were not, the incoherence that resulted impeded productive work and successful implementation of the reform. In Long Beach, for example, differences in hiring practices for "specialized" and "nonspecialized" positions led principals to game the system by moving teachers from one position to another in order to retain more control over hiring decisions. This undermined the district's effort to balance teaching quality across schools.

Achieving coherence in both the organizational elements and strategic priorities was especially challenging given the size and complexity of these large, urban districts. Clearly, this cannot happen without deliberate effort and attention. In fact, each of the districts we studied had created a role for *intermediaries,* district administrators who coordinated work with the schools. Although these individuals had different titles (e.g., area/community/zone/regional superintendents, executive directors, and network specialists), they were expected to broker, facilitate, or monitor the activities that were of greatest importance to both the central office and schools. Often they met with principals to interpret and monitor the expectations of central officials. Sometimes they recast requirements from the central office in order to increase the likelihood that principals would follow through. At other times they delivered bottom-up feedback from principals to the central office about whether a program or activity was working and, if not, how it might be improved. For example, in Baltimore, the intermediary executive directors coached principals about how to effectively manage their budgets and hire teachers in order to support a rigorous academic program. In short, intermediaries were agents of coherence.

We first draw on experiences in Aldine and Charlotte-Mecklenburg to illustrate the importance of achieving coherence among the organizational elements of resources, structures, and systems. Next, we provide examples from all five districts to show how the strategic priorities (budgeting, staffing, and the academic program) can be mutually reinforcing and thereby support the district's strategy.

Finally, we focus on the role that intermediaries played in helping the districts achieve coherence in practice.

THREE ORGANIZATIONAL ELEMENTS

The three main organizational elements that operate in the relationship between the central office and schools—resources, systems, and structures—interact in dynamic, sometimes unpredictable ways. For example, when a district cuts its budget, the reduction in resources may lead to larger classes and fewer teaching positions. This affects recruitment, hiring, placement, and layoffs because the district may have less need to recruit external candidates for teaching positions yet will have to carefully place current teachers who have lost their positions but hold tenure. Meanwhile, layoffs and transfers among less-experienced teachers may disrupt stability within some schools. In another example, changing a teacher evaluation system so that principals conduct more formal observations alters both the principal's role and how limited time can be used. As they commit scarce hours to writing and submitting evaluation reports, principals may spend less time talking informally with parents and teachers, an activity that develops community within the school. These changes in the principal's role and responsibilities may influence who aspires to become a principal and, consequently, how the district adjusts its system for leadership development.

Many district leaders tend to overlook the extent to which decisions about resources, systems, and structures overlap and interact. The district's organization chart, which sets forth the structures and formal relationships of the system, may seem like a manageable place for a new superintendent to begin making changes, and many do start there. However, the roles represented by the chart are ultimately tied to the district's supervisory and accountability systems. Changing the arrangement of departments or divisions or redefining the position of a deputy superintendent will affect how principals are held accountable in the district. Structural changes are also likely to change how resources are allocated. Changes such as these are not easy to anticipate, yet increasing coherence depends on being able to do so.

DIFFERENT DEGREES OF COHERENCE IN ALDINE AND CHARLOTTE-MECKLENBURG

Aldine proved to achieve high levels of coherence in pursuing its strategy by deliberately coordinating both *how* changes were made and *what* those changes were. That is, leaders modified resources, systems, and structures in ways that reinforced the district's strategy and made it more likely that principals would implement changes. Yet, Charlotte-Mecklenburg, where district leaders pursued a strategy for improvement that was grounded in predictions about the benefits of decentralization, did not always, and in some instances could not, ensure that the *how* and the *what* of their reforms were compatible. Although clearly communicated, some of the new systems and structures in Charlotte-Mecklenburg ran into problems when implemented at the school level. We found that in some cases these new systems and structures did not reinforce the district strategy.

Although district leaders in Aldine and Charlotte-Mecklenburg did not use the terms *coherence* or *incoherence* in describing their intentions, challenges, or accomplishments, they did describe their efforts to align or coordinate the work of those in the central office and the schools. One approach was to ask principals to map their school improvement plans onto the district's overall priorities. In Charlotte-Mecklenburg, for example, Superintendent Gorman told principals that their school-based strategic plans needed to be aligned with district goals. A principal explained, "Right when Dr. Gorman came, that's the biggest thing that always sticks out to me. He came in with a focus on strategic plans and said 'align everything to that.' And so I take that to the school level and teach the teachers here that everything we do has to be aligned to the strategic plan." The strategic plan was treated as a "living document," according to the senior district leaders, because it would change and improve with feedback from principals and zone superintendents, thus leading to greater coherence between what the central office was doing and the supports provided the schools. Charlotte-Mecklenburg's CAO explained how the district's strategic plan helped align the schools' strategic plans: "It's not make-believe and pretend. And it's certainly not a shelf document. I mean, everything from every line of our budget is tied to a strategic plan initiative. So, I think we have huge alignment from the board's theory of action all the way to the school improvement plan and individual growth plan, and I think in a district this size that draws a lot of our success. So to me it is that alignment."

In Aldine, we heard a very similar explanation. Principals consistently spoke about the importance of aligning their school's approaches with the goals laid out by the board and district. A high school principal recalled that before Texas officials set standards and administered tests, the curriculum and instruction were poorly aligned: "I remember the times when everybody shut their door in an elementary classroom and taught whatever they wanted. I remember the lady teaching dinosaurs for months—and what good is that to a second grade student? It's important that we align what we have." He went on to praise the district's approach to aligning practices from kindergarten through twelfth grade in a set of elementary and secondary schools: "vertical alignment, all of the vertical teams, and then having that come together at the district level—I do think is extremely important."

Although Charlotte-Mecklenburg and Aldine had similar expectations for aligning strategic plans at the school and district levels, they differed in the level of coherence they achieved in this part of their strategies. Aldine's use of resources, its structures, and its systems largely worked together to achieve the alignment across grades and schools that district officials sought. In Charlotte-Mecklenburg, some of the resources, structures, and systems contradicted one another and impeded implementation of the district's strategy.

In Aldine, the systems used for academic programming—detailed scope-and-sequence guides and benchmark assessments and targets—supported the district's goal to improve students' performance on the state tests. One veteran principal who had left the district for a few years explained how the systems helped her students perform better. She said that, in the other school district, "lesson planning felt like a free-for-all without the benchmark targets, and I lost confidence that I was effectively preparing students to take the state's standardized assessment. I knew if I came back, I could help my students succeed again." The principals we interviewed praised the central office for providing these supports in academic programming so that their students could meet the targets on the state test.

Aldine's staffing systems, structures, and resources also cohered with the district's strategy. The district recruited nationally and internationally, focusing on individuals who were training for a career in teaching. Human resource administrators sought to find teachers who understood and were willing to implement curriculum as well as individuals whose backgrounds reflected those of the students. The result was a pool of qualified teacher candidates. In this way, staffing served as a sustaining mechanism for the district's goal to improve student performance in all schools.

In Charlotte-Mecklenburg, the resources, systems, and structures sometimes worked at cross purposes and therefore did not consistently reinforce the district's strategy. In 2009–2010 the district developed a four-year strategic plan that emphasized school site autonomy and accountability for principals. The goal, as stated by Superintendent Gorman, was to move Charlotte-Mecklenburg from "managed instruction" to "managed performance," which meant giving principals more autonomy while increasing their individual accountability for school performance. The logic was that the district could only hold principals accountable for student achievement if they were free to make their own decisions. Although the district required principals to incorporate components of the strategic plan in their school plans, there were some organizational elements that contradicted the new strategy. For example, the Freedom and Flexibility system was designed to give higher performing principals more autonomy over decisions in their schools. However, informal communication structures already gave high performing principals autonomy in their work. The new system seemed redundant to some of the principals we interviewed; they did not feel compelled to do anything differently once they attained Freedom and Flexibility status and instead used it to evade bureaucratic requests from the central office. According to one zone superintendent, "Freedom and Flexibility has emerged as a reason not to do something. It has not led to any new innovative practices."

The prevailing, informal practice was that Charlotte-Mecklenburg's zone superintendents did not interfere with what principals of higher performing schools decided or did. In fact, these principals suggested that they claimed even more autonomy than they were granted under the Freedom and Flexibility initiative. As one principal observed, "The best principals ask for forgiveness, rather than permission." Thus, Freedom and Flexibility appeared to have little impact on how the district's plan to increase principals' autonomy was implemented. For the most part, principals did just what they'd been doing before.

Another system designed to give principals autonomy over staffing—the Strategic Staffing Initiative (SSI)—also had mixed results. SSI was a program that placed high performing principals in struggling schools, along with a team of five excellent teachers, an academic facilitator/director, and an assistant principal. Principals could invite effective teachers to join them in their new school, and those teachers would receive a $10,000 bonus in their first year and $5,000 retention bonuses at the end of their second and third years. Thus, financial and human resources were intended to support the strategy of relying on autonomous principals operating under heightened accountability to increase student learning. However, we found that the success of the system, again, depended on the informal networks that included only some principals. The principals who were very familiar with the schools and teachers in the district were far more successful in convincing effective teachers to accompany them to a struggling school. Meanwhile, principals who lacked deep familiarity and broad connections often were left scrambling as they tried to recruit teachers for the SSI in their new school.

For example, a middle school principal who was asked to take over a high school as part of the SSI could not recruit any of his current teachers due to differences between licensing requirements at middle and high schools. And because the principal did not have extensive contacts in high schools, he couldn't convince effective teachers from other high schools to transfer. According to this principal, the district denied several of his requests to move teachers because those teachers already were working at "needy" schools. In contrast, another SSI principal and former zone executive director successfully recruited teachers to join the staff at her new school. As zone executive director she had worked with many schools and easily could identify the best teachers in the zone. When she set out to recruit SSI teachers, she could rely on prior knowledge and relationships to successfully recruit five teachers, an assistant principal, and a literacy director. The problem was not that the SSI, as a formal system, favored some principals over others. Instead, there were no mechanisms beyond financial incentives to encourage effective teachers to change schools. Therefore, only those principals with informal districtwide networks could succeed. A lack of coherence among the resources, systems, and structures used to implement the SSI impeded the district's plan to improve low performing schools by giving principals a greater say in who taught there.

Attempts to give principals more autonomy over hiring and dismissal were also thwarted in Charlotte-Mecklenburg by staffing placement processes and informal group dynamics among principals. When we visited, the district was in its second year of implementing a reduction in force (RIF). When positions were cut, nontenured teachers (those with fewer than four years' experience) were the first to be laid off. Then, in a new process, tenured teachers were excessed from their schools based on their students' annual growth scores and placed in a districtwide pool. This resulted in a group of unsuccessful tenured teachers whom the district still had to place. Again, the placement process inhibited the move to give principals more control over who taught in their school. This example also illustrates an unintended consequence of the managed performance approach. Because managed performance also meant monitoring, rewarding, and penalizing teachers based on their performance, the system increased the role of the central office in staffing schools, thereby further constraining principals' influence over staffing decisions.

HOW ACCOUNTABILITY AND MONITORING SYSTEMS SUPPORT THE STRATEGIC PRIORITIES

As we explored the relationship between the central office and the schools in our five districts, we could see how their approach to resources, systems, and structures either supported or disrupted the relationships among academic programming, budgeting, and staffing. We use the example of accountability and monitoring systems, such as benchmarking, interim, and common assessments, to show how these elements guided principals' decisions about staffing and budgeting. If principals have data that students are struggling with a particular concept, they can provide professional development to teachers in that area or purchase supplementary materials to address the need. In this way, principals can use accountability and monitoring systems to inform decisions about staffing and budgeting.

Each district had some form of accountability and monitoring system. Although all were intended to track academic performance across a large number of schools, districts differed in how they used the data. Long Beach, for example, used a common end-of-course and quarterly assessment system to promote consistent academic programming across its schools. It paired curriculum guides with the assessment system. According to Superintendent Steinhauser and the deputy superintendent, this gave district administrators and principals access to data and pacing guides that they could then use to coordinate staffing and academic programming in the schools. Steinhauser noted, "We have a really nice data system . . . that our research office has set up that gives schools access to the various formative assessment data, drilled down to the individual teachers." A middle school principal in Long Beach explained how that assessment system helped her make decisions about the instructional activities in her school: "On a monthly basis, they sit down just like we're sitting right here, and my whole math department has their common assessment and they go around and they talk about their results." Teachers' discussions of their students' results on common assessments also served as an opportunity to share effective instructional practices. The principal explained, "They say, 'Well, what did you do differently this year? How did you do that?' And they're sharing best practice, and they're also sharing their frustrations. So it's a very great measure for me—an indicator of how we're doing so I can track our growth and know I'm on track."

An elementary school principal also spoke in support of the common assessment system and how it facilitated coherence between academic programming and staffing in his school: "We have common assessments; that's a critical component of our curriculum, common assessments aligned to the standards, based on the pacing." He said that the "vast majority" of the teachers "do follow the pacing . . . And I think that alone probably keeps some alignment on what's happening from school to school." Principals could often see which teachers were not following the curriculum by looking at the results of the common assessments, and low scores triggered a conversation. In Long Beach, the system gave principals information about the progress of student learning and the efficacy of teachers.

Montgomery County also had a well-developed accountability and monitoring system in place at the time of our visit. From the deputy superintendent's point of view, the systems "lay the groundwork" for coordinating the academic program and staffing practices in schools. The district had set an overall goal of college readiness, which was tied to students' average scores on the SAT and ACT. They then mapped the curriculum back to prekindergarten and established benchmark targets for seven key transition points, such as third grade reading proficiency and eighth grade algebra passing rates. The Office of School Performance—an important structure in implementing the district's strategy for improvement—then monitored whether schools were meeting the specified benchmarks. The district had developed a Monitoring Calendar with specific data points, targets, and questions that community superintendents could use when they met with principals to review their students' progress.

However, when we interviewed Superintendent Josh Starr, he expressed some concern about the role the monitoring system played in the district. He thought Montgomery County might have overemphasized accountability at the expense of innovation and establishing "psychological safety," the condition under which people are willing to share ideas and take risks without the fear of being harshly judged.[1] Starr described nascent plans to revise the system and, by doing so, to promote changes in the types of individuals the district recruited, hired, and promoted for leadership positions: "My expectation is that if it is very clear about what our work is here around helping people improve their practice then we will be able to identify who knows that and who's able to do it. I'm also going to bring in people and identify people who know how to do it."

At the school level, early changes in Montgomery County's assessment system met with some confusion when they reached the schools. In a departure from past practices, the central office had given schools some choice over the type of math assessment used for the accountability and monitoring system. One principal said that the district was changing the way students would be assessed in math, but central officials had not decided what approach they would use. He suggested that this indecisiveness had led schools across the district to try using different assessment systems: "So you've got a third of us who are trying to see how we can fuse the old system with the new system so we can have a transition. You got a third of the people who . . . immediately jumped on to the new thing without any kind of hesitation, and you have people who are in the middle, who are trying to do a little bit of both. So . . . what's the direction on it?"

These changes to the assessment and monitoring system in Montgomery County offer insight into what happens as a district attempts to alter its organizational elements to accommodate an amended theory of change. Josh Starr pursued a strategy that diminished the role of monitoring and accountability in the district. He predicted that different approaches to developing supports for teachers might serve students better than monitoring their learning and holding principals accountable for the results. Giving schools choice over the type of assessment used in the system led to confusion for some of the principals we interviewed. It was not clear whether the change diminished the feelings of apprehension and fear that Starr intended to address.

When we visited Aldine, the district had mandated the use of a detailed curriculum that had been mapped on to the Texas Essential Knowledge and Skills (TEKS) standards as well as the state test. It included "non-negotiable" guides for teachers that set forth six weeks of scope and sequence, including benchmark targets and comprehensive assessments. The benchmark targets, which described what a student should know and be able to do in nearly every course at every level, linked directly to relevant state standards. As a result, the assessments indicated whether a teacher was teaching the right topics in the right way at the right time. In this way, the Aldine benchmark monitoring system encouraged principals to make budgeting and staffing decisions that supported meeting the benchmark targets. For example, principals tended to favor hiring and retaining teachers who would closely follow the scope-and-sequence guides because they thought that the students of such teachers would do well on the benchmarking assessments. Superintendent Bamberg explained why the system of assessments was so important to principals as they tried to coordinate teachers' efforts. Without benchmark assessments, she said, if a principal is "not paying close attention" or "not truly attuned," he might mistakenly think that "everything's fine," even though the second grade teachers were not teaching the basics of fractions, which would affect students' scores on third grade tests—"the kids are going to fail the benchmark or they're going to fail some other school test." Eventually, scores on the state test would be low. She said that "the reason that we hold so dearly to our benchmarks" is that central administrators will be alerted to the problem, since the school could not create a substitute test to hide the shortcoming.

From the deputy superintendent's perspective, the benchmarking assessment system provided the only way to ensure coherence of curriculum, instruction, and teachers' skills and knowledge: "I hear it all the time, 'Teaching to the test.' We don't teach to the test, but if you're being assessed on something, you'd better focus on it. What is it you want me to do? Teach them this but test them on that? Well, come on. That doesn't make any sense."

Still, some principals thought that Aldine allowed the benchmark assessments and state exam to drive too many decisions about teaching and learning. One middle school principal lamented that the emphasis on state test scores diminished creative instruction by teachers: "A lot of the teacher talents, a lot of the teacher creativity cannot be expressed to the fullest because you have constraints when it comes to time, making sure that you fit all of these things in that the state says will be tested at the end of the year." Similarly, an elementary school principal thought getting all students to reach proficient levels on the state test took attention away from other, equally important educational matters: "I have probably about six, seven kindergarten students that are going through the mental health system for psychosis, bipolar, and you've got Mom [who] doesn't know what to do. It's draining. It's a lot. But I think that sometimes we get so focused on . . . 'Are you at 90 percent in reading? Are you at 90 percent in math?' that we forget about the child's needs and other things that the school may need, other than academics."

These examples from Aldine raise an interesting puzzle. Paradoxically, when there is a high degree of alignment and coherence in the strategic priorities that make up the strategy, that may constrain professional judgment or prevent pursuing other important work. In Aldine, the drive to excel on the state exam left two principals we interviewed wondering whether some students' needs were being ignored. This suggests that central administrators might have benefited from hearing these principals' concerns and adjusting the monitoring and accountability systems in response. In Aldine we also see the important distinction between coherence and conformity. A theory of change based on centralization and standardization does not always produce coherence. Coherence does not mean that principals do the same thing in every school every day. That is conformity and compliance, which discourage principals and teachers from tailoring the curriculum to meet their students' unique needs.

STRATEGIC PRIORITIES ARE INTERDEPENDENT

It was not enough for a district to coordinate how it relied on resources, systems, and structures to achieve its goals in budgeting, staffing, and academic programming; those strategic priorities also had to be compatible and mutually reinforcing. We found that whether the district's strategy was grounded in a theory of change that favored centralization or decentralization, decisions about budgeting had to enable and reinforce decisions about staffing and academic programming. If they didn't, the strategy was hampered by incoherence. For example, granting principals authority over hiring without providing them the resources (dollars, staff time, or training) needed to do a thorough job left the principals frustrated and led to a staff that had not been chosen with care. One obvious way in which the strategic priorities reinforced each other in these districts was in how budgeting supported decisions in academic programming and staffing. Again, Aldine and Charlotte-Mecklenburg illustrate how differences in budgeting decisions affected the other strategic priorities.

In Charlotte-Mecklenburg principals spoke of Superintendent Gorman's goal of having schools align budgeting decisions with their specific curricular and instructional needs. One high school principal recounted how he tried to link budgeting allocation decisions to the day-to-day instructional needs of the school through a weekly "ops" meeting with the department heads, assistant principals, head custodian, and financial secretary: "I am from the military, so I was already used to making budget decisions based on how they aligned with goals in the field. Gorman brought that kind of thinking to our district. At my school, I have a weekly meeting where we align and streamline all our decisions so they are resource-wise and support instruction in the classroom and align with the district's plan. We then e-mail those meeting minutes out to everybody—to the entire staff, so everyone knows that these decisions are aligned with our plan."

The challenge that these administrators faced as they tried to coordinate decisions about budgeting and academic programming was that they had limited control over their budget because North Carolina distributes resources for professional appointments as staffing units, not dollars, and because the funds with the fewest restrictions—local funds and Title I funding—were mostly in the control of the central office. The rationale for centralizing local funds was that district officials did not want principals to rely on such a volatile funding source for their academic programming decisions. Some Title I funding is centralized to pay for support teams that are assigned and supervised by zone superintendents. We found that the Title I funding that principals did have control over was substantial but came with strings attached, and approval to use them could take months. The end result was that principals had little sense of control over their resources. One principal described the buckets of money he had discretion over in his school: "You have money like the money that comes in from your vending machines and those kinds of monies that go into your checkbook. And then you have your instructional funds that you can use to buy all your instructional materials. Pencils, pens, copy machine, workbooks, and those types of things."

There is a stark contrast between the experiences of principals in Charlotte-Mecklenburg and in Aldine, where principals had nearly complete autonomy over their Title I budgets, which could reach nearly $1 million for larger high schools. They could thus make decisions in budgeting that addressed their school's staffing and academic programming needs. One high school principal described how she could budget her Title I funds to select the type of teacher and pedagogical approach she wanted in her school: "Now, through Title I, we hire about fourteen teachers . . . and I think that's very important when you're looking at struggling schools—that they prioritize the child . . . You have got to have people that prioritize the child." Similarly, an Aldine middle school principal described how he used a rigorous process to ensure that his budgeting decisions met his school's needs in academic programming and staffing: "With that right comes the responsibility of making sure that we're using our funds wisely and that we achieve some good things for students with the money that we have."

As these examples illustrate, the strategic priorities are interdependent; a change in one affects the others. By now it should be clear that working toward coherence was not simply about reaching uniformity in practice across schools. Rather, it required a differentiated approach that gives principals independence to meet the needs of their schools while meeting common systemwide expectations.

HOW INTERMEDIARIES SHAPE COHERENCE

We found one role that had the potential to increase coherence between the central office and the schools—the intermediary. Intermediaries had different titles. In Aldine they were called "area superintendents," in Baltimore "executive directors" and "network specialists," in Charlotte-Mecklenburg "zone superintendents," in Long Beach "assistant superintendents," and in Montgomery County "community superintendents." Nevertheless, these positions all were dedicated to bridging the organizational distance between the central office and the schools. The individuals who held them often served as crucial brokers delivering information about what the system expected, offering support to principals so that they could function effectively in the system, and conveying feedback to central administrators from the schools' principals, parents, and teachers.

The role of intermediaries has garnered attention from others studying the relationship between central offices and schools in large urban districts. For example, a report by McKinsey & Company draws attention to the importance of this "middle layer" in the world's highest performing school systems.[2] The report's authors found that these leaders in the middle acted as integrators and mediators between schools and central office, facilitating communication and collaboration, providing targeted support, and buffering local resistance to policy changes. Meredith Honig and colleagues at the Center for the Study of Teaching and Policy at the University of Washington reached similar conclusions in studying central office transformation. In a series of influential reports and articles, they describe how intermediaries can act as instructional leaders by actively coaching principals to improve teaching and learning in their schools.[3]

We, too, found that the intermediaries in the districts we studied played important roles in moving the system toward greater coherence. They communicated to teachers and principals important information about curricular changes, human resource policies, assessment procedures, and special events. They also played key roles in making the accountability systems in the districts work. However, the span of responsibility, the level of influence, and the focus of intermediaries' work varied widely, and in some cases their roles remained in flux.

In Aldine, the job of the area superintendent was straightforward: prevent school-level problems from rising to the superintendent, monitor student achievement and implementation of curriculum, deploy additional supports to struggling schools, and serve as a buffer between the central office and the schools. Their ultimate responsibility was to ensure consistency of implementation across the system, particularly in curriculum and assessment. In carrying out these duties, area superintendents used support and encouragement to convince principals to act in ways that would facilitate coordination across the system. For example, the area superintendents translated central office policies into terms more amenable to the principals and then developed a communication plan to gain the principals' commitment. One area superintendent explained how she and her colleagues would develop such a plan in cabinet meetings: "Someone or something says, 'You must go forth and do this.' The area superintendents will meet together, and we say, 'Okay, well how are we going to get this out? Let's come up with a plan so that when it goes out it's consistent and we're all saying the same thing.' And then we turn it into a positive. And that's how we expect the principals to take something that's hard and give it to their staff [so that they don't say,] 'The superintendent said that la la la la la.'"

When we visited Baltimore in the spring of 2012, the district was making a significant change in how it structured its intermediary roles. In three years the district had moved from having two executive directors overseeing 200 schools to having 16 school networks, each with 8–15 schools. The new structure was intended to address the tensions that often arose between providing accountability and support for principals. One administrator in each network—called an executive director—assumed most of the responsibility for holding principals accountable. Meanwhile, a network team composed of a facilitator and representatives from central office departments (e.g., special education, human resources, curriculum and instruction) provided assistance and support. CEO Alonso and his senior leaders found that it was difficult for an executive director to simultaneously hold principals accountable and help them; they reportedly could do one or the other, but not both. So, the network–executive director structure emerged.

However, the executive directors said that they still struggled with their role even with the new network structure. The district invested resources in coaching the executive directors about how to deliver feedback and have productive conversations with principals. At the time of our visit, the roles of executive director and facilitator had started to blend. For example, an executive director might work closely with a new principal to design a comprehensive school improvement plan. Then the executive director and principal would work together with the facilitator and network team to implement the plan. As one senior district leader said, "The plans that they [executive directors] come up with [with] the principal, the facilitator and the principal work to implement."

In Montgomery County, the role of the intermediary was also changing, and that change substantially affected the resources and systems in the academic program, especially assessment. As Superintendent Starr tried to shift the district's orientation from an emphasis on monitoring and accountability to one of support and development, he initially enacted the change through the role of the community superintendent. Starr increased the number of community superintendents and asked them to spend at least 70 percent of their time in schools. His goal was to shift community superintendents from brokering and monitoring to supporting and coaching. However, there were immediate challenges in the reorientation. Community superintendents had no formal authority to grant resources to the principals who needed more support. At the same time, the position's formal responsibilities still emphasized monitoring and accountability. Starr explained the problems he encountered as he tried to reorient the community superintendent's role: "It seemed to me like they were sort of in this limbo where they were monitoring, but they didn't really seem to have—or feel that they have—the authority to actually make decisions or allocate resources. They also didn't know a lot of the things that were going on in some of their schools or some of the various initiatives . . . If the idea is that we want to support principals, then the people who are directly supervising them need to have some authority . . . They certainly didn't feel that they had it and a lot of people questioned what their job was, so, 'What do they do? Do they just come and monitor us with checklists?'"

For their part, the community superintendents also were trying to understand their new role. One reflected on Starr's expectation that they would deeply understand their assigned schools and develop strong relationships with principals: "You have to have a relationship there hopefully where they trust you, [where] you can sit down. If they've got a problem, they're willing to work through it with you." He said that it was important to assign community superintendents a reasonable number of schools so that "they don't feel like you're either too busy because you're just there to check off a box . . . that you're only concerned with documenting something for an evaluation."

The reality of limited resources suggested that achieving familiar, well-informed, and respectful relationships between community superintendents and principals would be difficult; the ratio of schools to community superintendent was still about 40 to 1. One community superintendent doubted that he could achieve the kind of one-to-one relationship that Starr envisioned under the current ratio: "The challenge, I think, is if you want to have that type of relationship and focus, how do you do that when you have thirty-six schools? . . . I guess there's that type of capacity piece."

In Charlotte-Mecklenburg, the roles and responsibilities of the zone superintendents were left largely undefined. This seemed to result in a situation where personal relationships, sometimes influenced by political alliances and preferences, determined central office–school interactions. Principals talked about how the individual zone superintendents' philosophies of leadership and personal experiences determined whether they were effective. Some zone superintendents were said to be hands-off, while others micromanaged. Some were "strict," and others were "respectful." Principals were more affected by the personal inclinations of their zone superintendent than by the features of the role itself. One principal said, "It's strictly according to the leadership style of that zone superintendent. [One zone superintendent] believed in his principals and his principals did their work . . . There are other zone superintendents who believe it's their job to tell principals what to do, because they are more traditional in their style. So it's strictly dependent upon your zone superintendent." Thus, the central office–schools relationship in Charlotte was largely determined by the particular style of the zone superintendent. Some zone superintendents visited the schools on a regular basis, others only once or twice a year. One principal explained, "It's a trust level that you have with your area sup. I would tell him . . . 'I want to do this and this.' So even though I didn't have Freedom and Flexibility, you know, when I talked my zone superintendent through this idea, he said, 'How is this going to work?' I explained it to him, and he gave me the green light."

These examples from Aldine, Baltimore, Montgomery County, and Charlotte-Mecklenburg raise important questions about the ideal roles and responsibilities of intermediaries. In Aldine, the area superintendents moderated central office mandates to be sure that they would be implemented, and they buffered the central office from the less important problems that occurred at the school level. In Baltimore and Montgomery County, the intermediaries tried to reconcile the tension between holding principals accountable and giving them support. In Charlotte-Mecklenburg, the role was loosely defined and subject to personal preferences and alliances.

Many leaders in these districts were thoughtful about how to strike the right balance between accountability and support in the intermediary's role. The important lesson is that balancing that tension is only one part of managing for coherence. Appointing a skilled staff member to an intermediary position only promoted improvement in instruction and learning when it enabled the resources, systems, and structures to work together toward achieving a strategic goal. If the intermediary did not have authority to modify a faulty system, then principals resorted to workarounds that made it even more difficult for district officials to manage for coherence.

SUMMARY

In illustrating practical coherence (and incoherence) in the central office–schools relationship, we examined the three organizational elements and the three strategic priorities. We learned that when resources, systems, and structures work together harmoniously, it is possible to advance the district strategy. Academic programming, budgeting, and staffing are also interdependent; increasing coherence means the priorities reinforce, rather than contradict or undermine, each other. Finally, a role such as area superintendent can play a beneficial role in shaping coherence in the district; however, districts face the challenge of limiting the number of principals each intermediary works with and deciding how to separate, balance, or integrate the evaluative and coaching aspects of that role.

Resources, systems, and structures are important elements of the working relationship between the central office and the schools. However, their coordination and ultimate effectiveness depend on how principals carry out their work in the schools.

LESSONS FOR PRACTICE

⊃ *Budgeting, staffing, and academic programming are interdependent; changes in one are very likely to affect the others, even if it you can't immediately see the effects.* As you consider changes, carefully explore how they will work, possibly by drawing together a diverse group of school-based and central administrators and teachers to review and critique a proposed change. Their responses are likely to identify unanticipated—but very real—problems, and together they may devise possible solutions.

⊃ *Although structure may be the most obvious leverage point for improving coherence and performance, it is not the only one.* Although superintendents often move quickly to change the district's structures, such changes are unlikely to improve practice without complementary changes in systems and resources. Public education leaders would do well to use caution in making structural changes, since these actions alone may go no further than redesigns of the organization chart.

⊃ *Always start with a clear theory of change and strategy.* As the Cheshire Cat says, "If you don't know where you are going, any road will take you there." The theory of change and strategy should drive ongoing decisions about the strategic priorities and organizational elements. Without a clear idea about why and how changes are being made, achieving coherence will be left to chance.

⊃ *Recognize the potential of intermediary positions to increase coherence between the central office and the schools.* Intermediaries can do much more than deliver and enforce top-down expectations from district administrators to those in the schools. With varying degrees of coaching and oversight, intermediaries can ensure that the organization will improve performance while continuing to develop.

⟩ *Consider the demands and capacity of the intermediary role and the developmental needs of individuals who hold it.* It's unrealistic for intermediaries to serve a large number of schools in anything but the most perfunctory way. Therefore, having a reasonable span of control is essential. However, it's not enough just to create such a role, for the demands of coaching or supervising principals require intermediaries to have sophisticated personal skills and deep organizational understanding. Therefore, district officials need to establish a system for training these individuals if they are to facilitate coherence.

FOUR

Engaging Principals as Partners, Advocates, and Adversaries

Principals often are said to be the key to a school's success—"Show me a great school and I'll show you a great principal." From the perspective of those in the central office, principals are the district's crucial insiders who lead teachers in instructional improvement, build and maintain community support for public education, and successfully manage an array of programs consistent with district policy. They are vital agents in the district's effort to implement its strategy for instructional improvement.

At the same time, though, principals champion their own school's program, enhance its reputation, and secure the money and materials needed for education to thrive in its classrooms. Because teachers and parents see the principal as their school's primary advocate who brokers relationships and secures resources on their behalf, they are quick to criticize if their principal seems to put the district's interests ahead of their school's. They believe that an effective principal stands up to those "downtown." Principals, therefore, simultaneously serve two masters and manage the often-competing expectations of central office administrators and their school's constituents.

Things go well when the interests of the school and those of the central office line up. However, when they diverge, the principal's primary allegiance may well be to his school. In making key decisions that might seem to pit the school against the district, a superintendent must keep all schools in mind. A principal, however, is likely to think first about his own school.

PRINCIPALS ARE SCHOOL-BASED STAKEHOLDERS

Principals, therefore, often play the role of stakeholder in the very system that employs them. District officials who operate high up in the district's bureaucracy may choose programs, allocate funds, and issue rules and regulations, but it is principals and their teachers who interact with students and families as "street-level bureaucrats."[1] Day to day, they shape how the work is done within their school and classrooms. They monitor the possible effects of central office proposals and decisions on their school, often using their position, reputation, and political sway to do whatever it takes to serve their students well.

Critics sometimes suggest that if principals do not toe the line drawn by central administrators, they should be reprimanded and, if need be, dismissed. Yet, it would be a mistake for central office administrators to ignore their principals' concerns or advocacy, for to do so would mean missing crucial information or insights about how their policies or practices are working once they reach schools and classrooms. Valuable advice about how to improve the district's strategy would be lost. As discussed in chapter 2, the district's plans and decisions are better if they are informed and enhanced by those in the schools whose work they are meant to affect. However, reciprocal influence between central and school leaders not only strengthens implementation of key decisions and programs but also builds a foundation of trust that is crucial for a district's academic success. For if district administrators demand top-down compliance, they may find that principals subsequently fail to support—or may even actively oppose—key elements of the district's improvement strategy.

However, if district leaders take the varied needs and interests of principals and their schools into account, they can gain steady support for their strategy.

In many large urban districts, the relationship between principals and central administrators is marked by distrust. Sometimes they are locked in rancorous conflict, but more often each side is skeptical of the other's motives and commitment. Often, central administrators expect principals to "get with the program" and principals, in turn, feign compliance while continuing to go their own way. One feature that seemed to distinguish the districts we studied from many others is that principals generally suggested that their interests were consistent with those of central office administrators, rather than being at odds. However, most principals were neither passive nor routinely compliant. They sometimes acted as advocates to maintain or expand their school's share of decision-making rights. They occasionally encouraged their constituents or colleagues to support or ignore a directive from the central office. And at times they gamed the system, selectively using the district's rules and resources to their school's advantage. Tensions sometimes ran high when district officials unilaterally changed the rules in order to improve the system's performance. And principals sometimes contested new restrictions on their autonomy, arguing that the district's plans or proposals would undermine, rather than enhance, their school's effectiveness.

Notably, however, principals also accepted the need for their district to respond effectively to recent demands for accountability and unanticipated cuts in state and local funding. They were less likely to resist or confront those in the central office than they might have been two decades ago, when the environment of public education was more settled and predictable. For their part, district officials rarely suggested that principals were their adversaries. Both groups seemed to realize that their fortunes were interdependent and that the success of each depended on the good-faith actions of the other. In fact, as principals pursued their school-based interests, they tended to work in partnership with central office officials. When they were dissatisfied, they did not hunker down in opposition but remained engaged. They continued to make their best case on behalf of their school's teachers, parents, and students, while central officials calculated how to build and maintain support for the district's strategy, by gaining principals' genuine endorsement or at least their tacit acceptance of the district's policies and practices.

Here we explore the interests, interactions, and tensions that played out between principals and central office administrators as these five districts allocated funds; hired, assigned, and reassigned teachers; and implemented curricula and student assessments. Of the three strategic priorities we studied, decisions about the budget and staffing generated more central office–schools tension than did decisions about the academic program.

Budget Cuts and Centralized Funding Fuel Central Office–Schools Tensions

School districts spend money on an enormous range of services, but the resources that most directly affect teaching and learning are those that pay for salaries and benefits for instructional staff (teachers, specialists, and paraprofessionals) as well as subsidize various supports for their work, such as curricula, textbooks, technology, and professional development. Because these instructional funds are critical to students' success, both the district and the schools have an interest in how much money is available, how it is spent, and who decides how to spend it.

The school budgets in these five districts included funds from various sources. Largest and most important were the basic grants from local and state governments, which might be allocated to schools using a per-pupil or weighted student formula. Supplementing these was compensatory funding for schools in low-income communities, including categorical grants from programs such as federal Title I or comparable state-level programs, which were given directly to eligible schools or disbursed strategically by the central office to meet districtwide needs. In addition, some schools benefited from the proceeds of fund-raising by PTAs or school-based foundations.

Over the past fifteen years, the magnitude and mix of these resources has changed in these districts, leaving schools located in all types of communities—high income, middle income, and low income—with less money and less control over how it can be spent.

Only in Baltimore did principals recently gain greater autonomy over the use of funds from basic and categorical grants. We can't say whether students benefited more from one approach or the other, but we can say that when district officials reduced or reclaimed control of compensatory funds, their actions strained relationships between principals and central office administrators.

Across the five districts, most central office administrators sought to align the available funds with the district's strategy for improvement and tried to allocate resources fairly and efficiently so that students in all schools would have access to good instruction and a fair chance to succeed. However, given the wide range of economic conditions in the communities these schools served, all superintendents faced the challenge of effectively meeting and fairly addressing those demands. Principals of schools in low-income communities argued that their students' greater needs warranted extra resources. Those heading more affluent schools acknowledged the challenges that their colleagues in low-income schools faced, but they also lobbied for more funds to support their own school's special programs and priorities.

Basic Funding. The districts used different approaches to allocate basic funding to the schools. Facing questions about what a school's fair share of the district resources should be, superintendents necessarily had to consider whether funding students with equal dollars meant that all those students would be well served. Each district had its own rationale for its approach to funding and the implications that approach had for equity.

Three districts (Aldine, Long Beach, and Montgomery County) relied on straightforward per-pupil funding. Long Beach superintendent Chris Steinhauser explained that the numbers of enrolled students determined a school's allocation: "It's all based on FTE [full-time equivalent] and the same dollar amount per kid." Implicit in such explanations was the belief that per-pupil funding was, in itself, fair or that subsequent grants to low-income schools could be added to ensure greater equity. Two districts (Baltimore and Charlotte-Mecklenburg) addressed issues of equity by allocating more money to schools that served students with greater needs.

Charlotte-Mecklenburg superintendent Peter Gorman explained his district's scheme: "If you live in poverty as a student, you are allocated [at a rate of] 1.3. So, imagine you've got two schools with 1,000 children; one is 100 percent free and reduced lunch. We staff that school for 1,300 kids. If we have a school that has no poverty, we staff that school as though it had 1,000 kids. Well, 30 percent more staff, 30 percent more supply budget—that adds up."

Gorman explained that with recent budget cuts, this approach had drawn complaints from school-site stakeholders as resources became increasingly "lean in our suburban schools. We're starting to get the first push and backlash from our parent communities." He recalled one principal from a higher-income school protesting: "I know we said, 'We're all in this together,' and I was with you as long as we had a science resource teacher," but losing the science resource teacher had undermined his support for the district's funding formula. Notably, in Baltimore, where dollars followed the student in a formula called Fair Student Funding, schools received more money to educate low-income students and those with disabilities. Also, however, schools enrolling students scoring at the top of student assessments received additional funds in order to ensure that schools attracting successful students had the means to continue doing so and, thus, to retain those students in the district.

Compensatory Funding. Additional state and federal funds from categorical programs such as Title I also helped local districts address the greater financial needs of schools serving low-income students. For example, although Aldine funded schools on a strict per-pupil basis, schools with concentrations of low-income students could decide how to spend their share of categorical funds. Principals there said that, until recently, a large portion of their budget came from federal Title I or state Compensatory Education funding. According to Superintendent Bamberg, Aldine annually received approximately $20 million in compensatory funds, of which "a good bit of that goes to the campuses. So that's when [low-income schools] can pick up additional math and reading people and science people." She acknowledged that the district "pulls some off the top that we use to give a skills specialist" to the schools that need one, "and then beyond that they can take the rest of their money and do what they want." Principals indicated that they appreciated having the right to decide. One explained that Title I funds made it possible "to hire about fourteen teachers" beyond what the school's basic per-pupil funding allowed. Another principal of a low-income Aldine school said, "I can use my Title I funds and that makes it equitable—more equitable." However, recent budget cuts had substantially reduced the state grants that low-income schools received. One Aldine principal explained, "Comp Ed was significantly cut. I had one-hundred-and-something-thousand dollars last year, and that was cut to $3,000."

In other districts, recent cuts in both basic and categorical funding meant that principals generally not only had fewer dollars to work with, but they also had less say in how they would be spent, causing considerable dissatisfaction among some. The move to centralize categorical funds had gone furthest in Long Beach, where Superintendent Steinhauser described how the shift in control was intended to increase equity: "We used to be very decentralized on that . . . And we now basically control all the categorical funds to address the strategic plan. That goes back to [providing] equity and access for everybody. And so the sites don't have much flexibility at all over their restricted categorical dollars because [those funds] basically have gone to support things that are important to the strategic plan . . . In the past, you would have one school that would spend all their money very well and another school that wouldn't spend it well at all . . . I believe centralization is a better way to go."

Similarly, Montgomery County decided to concentrate categorical funds on a smaller number of schools, and district officials—not principals—decided where those funds would be spent. A budget official said, "We have narrowed it down to fewer schools. So we served under thirty schools [with Title I dollars] for the past ten years, and this year it's twenty-eight . . . So you actually concentrate the Title I funding instead of dispersing it across a greater number of schools."

Schools that failed to qualify for compensatory funds sometimes relied on their PTA or local school foundation to supplement what they had; a few principals of wealthy schools said that they could raise enough money to fund extra teaching positions. One Montgomery County school's PTA sponsored several annual fund-raisers—a silent auction, a casino night, and a wine tasting. A Long Beach principal said that his school's parent foundation raised money from local businesses and corporations: "They write a lot of grants. And over the last three years, they've probably brought in close to $75,000 to $80,000 . . . Obviously it hasn't made up for the $250,000 [in basic funding] that we lost, but it has definitely helped us to shore up some programs that otherwise would have gone away." Although principals in Long Beach had no say in how categorical funds were spent, they controlled the use of dollars that their schools raised.

Principals faced substantial challenges if their school neither qualified for categorical funding nor had sufficient wealth in their local community to make fund-raising feasible. A Charlotte-Mecklenburg principal explained that schools where only 30–65 percent of their students qualified for free and reduced-priced meals were in a "weird area, because you don't have the rich parents and then you don't have the governmental support. So you've pretty much got to be resourceful on your own for that." Superintendent Gorman described the bind he was in when he encouraged school-based fund-raising in higher-income schools: "Well, how do we quietly get them, through their PTA, to fundraise? And then we get folks in our more impoverished communities saying, 'That's unfair. [Parents in our school] can't afford that. Whatever they buy, you need to automatically give us.' And my response was, 'You might not realize this, but we've already given you that [through weighted student staffing].'"

How Much of Their Instructional Budgets Do Principals Actually Control?

For many of the principals we interviewed, having some control over their budget seemed nearly as important as the number of dollars they actually received. They suggested that when they had some say, they could be creative and agile, rather than feeling boxed in by their district's requirements. In the districts we studied, Baltimore principals had the most discretion over school-site budgeting and those in Long Beach had the least.

Under CEO Alonso's policy of bounded autonomy, Baltimore's principals took responsibility for building their budget, although they had to gain the parents' endorsement before submitting it to the district. Beyond being required to have a certain number of special educators at each school, Baltimore principals could—within broad guidelines—spend their money. One principal provided an example: "We have the opportunity to hire what they call 'temporary employees.' They may work full time, but they're not a Baltimore City union member. It doesn't come with the contracts and benefits . . . For example, I've hired parents who manage the cafeteria, who help with hall monitoring, who may help with making sure students are in uniform or call home for certain things." Baltimore principals valued having such discretion, which was not available to their counterparts in other districts. One Baltimore principal even said that he had applied for the position *because* of this new policy:

> That's what made me become interested in becoming a principal, because, prior to Dr. Alonso, I didn't want to have any dealings with the principalship because they seemed like puppets. They couldn't even control their budget. To me, you're not the principal, or you're not the head of any organization, if you don't have the final say on how you spend your money. I don't care if the budget is $10,000; I want to say how I'm going to spend my $10,000 . . . because [without that] you're holding me accountable for my test scores, and I think I know how to fix it, but I have to do it your way.

Central administrators in the other districts were far more prescriptive about how available funds could be spent and how closely they monitored the schools' allocations. One central administrator in Montgomery County said, "We actually staff every grade level in every school centrally . . . So, it's very formula driven, and principals have few opportunities to really make decisions about how they're going to use positions differently." A Montgomery County principal opposed this approach: "I would jump through a zillion hoops to say, 'I don't really need four counselors. I only need three and a half counselors, and I want to take that counseling position and put it into teachers' . . . It's those [district] directives of what they want to see in every school, to try to keep the [district] fairly equal—it's very difficult to make those changes."

Charlotte-Mecklenburg's central administrators also closely regulated the use of Title I funds, much to the consternation of some principals. One had welcomed the district's budgeting guidelines when she was a new principal; however, she said, "now I feel like it's more restrictive and I need to be able to do whatever I need to do, since I'm going to be held accountable for the results. So, I don't like really having to wait for [the district administrator] to say, 'Oh, it's okay. You get approval.' I want to spend my money and get the results I need to get. So, having still to answer to somebody else about how I may spend my money, when I can spend it, when I can access it, who I can and can't hire—that annoys me to no end." Another principal offered an example to explain his frustration: his school had been outfitted with a virtual lab, but he did not have "anybody to man it." Instead of paying a full-time media teacher to run the lab, he wanted to "take a half-time teacher position . . . and I can get an assistant that gets paid less [to run the lab] and then have a little money left over. So, I could have two people for a half-teacher position, and I could do what I needed to do." That would have been permitted in Baltimore but not in Charlotte-Mecklenburg. He acknowledged that because some principals couldn't manage such a complex process, the central office might have to say, "Hey, this is what you get." However, he resented the standardized allocation process and the limitations it placed on his efforts to stretch the dollars so that he could staff his school more effectively.

Similarly, Long Beach principals complained when Superintendent Steinhauser revoked their right to control Title I funds. A principal recalled, "Once upon a time, I had a budget, and then it got skinnier and skinnier and skinnier. And then two years ago they froze the budget and said, 'You have nothing.'" She went on to explain that "today, I just get doled out a very small, little allowance for paper and toilet paper and pencils and general supplies. And then for everything else the superintendent will give you a projected number of students and divide that by thirty-one [the standard class size], and that's the number of teachers that he's going to pay for. And you just have to make it work." She objected to the principal's subordinate role in the process. "So, he has the purse, and he's doling out the allowance to each of the different schools, depending on what he sees they need." She speculated that it would be "a long time" before principals might recover control of their budgets: "I get the impression that [central administrators] like the way it is."

Steinhauser suggested that this principal's response was not unusual: "That was the biggest complaint: 'What? You mean we don't just get to spend money how we want?' And the answer was, 'No, we're in fiscal anorexia, and if you have a choice between cheese and Cheetos, you're eating cheese, because we know that's a healthier option.'" He emphasized that the district was "totally going to support [the principals]" but that the "money is centralized. It's apportioned out by sites, but it needs my signature and [the associate superintendent's] signature to get spent." He said that the district required principals to submit "an agenda" for the allocations, including links to goals and objectives in their school's improvement plan. That, he said, "threw people for a loop . . . People were mad, really mad, because what you just basically did is you said, 'You get an allowance, not a salary.'"

Overall, these principals seemed to adjust—though reluctantly and, in some cases, resentfully—to their school's new financial circumstances and the restrictions imposed by district officials. No one suggested that the funds were being misused and, in fact, many expressed confidence that district administrators made their decisions with students' needs in mind. It was just that centralized decisions could not possibly account for the priorities, programs, and practices of so many different schools. In most cases, a basic level of trust in central office administrators cushioned the impact of these decisions. However, principals did object when they thought that their students and programs were hurt by moves to centralize budgeting. This raises the question of how a district can effectively manage scarce funds on behalf of all schools and students, while still encouraging the investment and initiative of successful principals who know their school's needs and want to control their own resources. That principal in Baltimore who applied for his job because it came with budgetary authority might well decide to leave if the central office suddenly reclaimed his dollars and ended his right to spend them as he saw fit.

PRINCIPALS WANT TO CHOOSE THEIR TEACHERS

Just as central office administrators must depend on principals to advance the district's vision and strategy, principals must depend on their teachers to succeed with students. One Long Beach principal echoed the views of many we interviewed: "I've always said, it's all about the teachers, all about the teachers, all about the teachers."

As with budgeting, several processes combine to determine the composition of a school's instructional staff—recruitment, hiring, tenure, layoffs, and reassignment. During periods of growth, principals concentrate on recruiting and hiring new teachers. However, when districts contract in size or face unexpected program cuts, principals' attention shifts to teacher layoffs and reassignment. Large urban districts routinely face teacher shortages in certain fields—special education, math, science, and foreign languages—and thus they continue to recruit and hire new teachers, whether the district is growing or not. However, because individual schools we studied also coped with program disruptions caused by budget cuts, principals paid close attention to state and local policies that affected layoffs and reassignment, including the teachers' contracts.

Charlotte-Mecklenburg's Strategic Staffing Initiative allowed principals who were reassigned to high-need schools to choose five high performing teachers from any school in the district to join them, whatever the seniority of those teachers might be. These principals appreciated having this lever that provided some control over staffing in their new, challenging school. However, because these principals chose highly successful teachers to join them, the schools those teachers left suffered their loss. Principals who understood and had mastered the complicated rules of teacher assignments did their best to use those rules to control who taught in their school. Others, however, seemed resigned to weather the inevitable impact of layoffs and reassignment, doing their best with what came their way.

Principals Value the District's Role in Recruiting and Screening Candidates

In all five districts, the central office recruited and screened pools of teaching candidates. Aldine, with one of the most ambitious programs, recruited teachers nationally and internationally. One principal explained, "Aldine is very proactive when it comes to making the partnerships with the universities all across the continental United States." Some candidates from other parts of the country even chose to do their student teaching in Aldine so that they would be familiar with the district's curriculum and be known by at least one school's principal and staff, all of which might work to their advantage in landing a job. As one principal explained, "That's why we have a lot [of new teachers] from Wisconsin, a lot from Iowa, and so on." She, like other Aldine principals, was satisfied with both the pool of candidates recruited and screened by district administrators and with the district's online system that made it possible to search for candidates who matched her school's needs.

We found that having access to thorough, accurate, and timely information was essential in order for school-based hiring to work well. Each year, Montgomery County received 8,000–9,000 applications from prospective elementary teachers but hired only 300. One principal described how, based on candidates' qualifications and references, district screeners assigned each applicant a "ranking score . . . 'highly recommend,' 'recommend,' and 'don't-even-look-at' kind of status." Principals appreciated the district's role in the process. As one said, "I'll vet the candidates with the support of HR . . . I can finally now see people's resumés online and see their background, which is great, whether I'm at home or here. You used to have to go up to central office and go through files."

Human resource administrators in Long Beach relied primarily on local sources for their applicant pool, especially California State

University at Long Beach, where teacher education students were required to give 120 hours of community service to the school system. Thus, principals would know many of the potential candidates and encourage the best to apply for openings at their school. Superintendent Steinhauser explained, "So they're in our classrooms, they're kind of learning the 'Long Beach Way.' We're getting to see them and kind of look at people that are really passionate about their work." Like other districts, Long Beach centrally reviewed candidates' formal credentials and screened for past felonies. They also administered a formal Haberman STAR interview, designed to identify teachers who will "succeed with even the most challenging student."[2] Then they made the names of promising candidates available to principals.

Although principals in these three districts expressed satisfaction with their district's centralized recruitment and screening process, those in Charlotte-Mecklenburg and Baltimore City—where schools had more autonomy in hiring—suggested that they did not have the assistance they needed. Principals of high-poverty, hard-to-staff schools faced extra demands due to repeated teacher turnover, and it was hard to do a thorough job of recruiting teachers from the main office of a school. When principals thought that the service they received from the central office fell short, they often had trouble finding the time or creating the connections that would yield a pool of strong candidates who fit their school's needs. One Charlotte-Mecklenburg principal said that she went through the process, asking central office to advertise and recruit candidates for an open position. But when she went down to the central office to look through a binder of candidates who had applied, she did not find any she wanted to interview: "I was unsuccessful. I didn't get one teacher through the process." Ultimately, the principal had to identify candidates through her own network and ask them to apply for the open position. Similarly, a Baltimore principal was dissatisfied with the district's centralized lists of candidates: "I don't always find those lists as effective . . . I seek out and recruit my own teachers, because I know what I'm looking for. We do have job fairs that will allow us to get support for teacher vacancies, but I kind of grow my own. I find a relationship with a college or university and I get students who are in their student teacher placements."

Principals Largely Control Hiring Decisions

Historically, the central office took responsibility for hiring the district's teachers and assigning them to schools that had openings. Increasingly, however, principals are doing the hiring after the central office screens the candidates. That was true in four of the districts we studied, although principals did not always have the right to consider all the candidates in the pool. For example, a central administrator in Montgomery County said, "We really do give principals a lot of freedom to pick. It's not like they can pick out of one hundred people, but they can pick the one person out of thirty." Aldine principals were required to maintain a racial and ethnic balance falling between 3 and 5 percent of the district's targets. A principal there said, "As the instructional leader and with site-based decision making, we select who we want. But when you go above that [percentage], you get a phone call [from HR]." Principals in Charlotte-Mecklenburg were required to interview a certain number of candidates before hiring one, but they could choose who that one would be. As a principal there explained, "We have the final say on that, which is good, because you've got to find somebody that's going to fit in with your culture and team."

Various principals described the school-based process that they used to interview and hire from a pool of screened candidates. A number relied on teams of teachers and parents to jointly interview candidates and recommend their choice to the principal, who ultimately decided. They underscored the benefits of having teachers and parents scrutinize candidates during school visits, including observing prospective teachers' instruction to see if they knew their subject well and seemed to engage that school's students in learning. An Aldine principal explained why he wants to see candidates interact with students: "Our kids are not going to work for you until they know you care about them and you love them. And if you don't establish that connective tissue piece first, they will never work for you." Some principals also wanted to gauge whether candidates were likely to become good colleagues with current staff. A careful selection process demanded time from all involved, but when it worked well, new teachers began their jobs having some allegiance to their school, their principal, and their fellow teachers.

Several districtwide factors affected the timetable for posting jobs and hiring new staff. The union contract typically required that all tenured teachers be assigned positions before new ones were hired. Delays in approving state or municipal budgets could push hiring decisions back into July or August, when current teachers were on vacation and unavailable to interview candidates. For example, in 2011 Montgomery County hired 832 teachers after July 1. Most teachers were hired by their principal based on paper qualifications and an in-person interview. Principals said that effective recruitment and screening by their central office made it possible for them to make good decisions at that late stage of the process, but this delay also meant that the new teachers' colleagues would not know them in advance or be prepared to support their successful induction.

In contrast to those four districts, Long Beach hired teachers centrally. Still, district officials kept principals' preferences in mind. A central administrator described the local process, which Long Beach principals generally endorsed:

> There's definitely opportunity for [the principal] to recommend someone back to HR, but there's no decentralized offering of contract, or anything like that. It's all a centralized function . . . [The candidates] are background-vetted, and then, in the best of times, when we were actually hiring people, the staffer might give the principal five names and say, "Now, you're welcome to choose from this pool of candidates. These have all taken the Haberman [interview]. They've all been recommended." And then the principal can interview, either with a panel or him- or herself, and then make a recommendation back to HR. But it's been made pretty clear: when you're interviewing, you're not offering [a job] to the person.

There is some advantage when the principal can offer a job to a new teacher, because that exchange reinforces the bond between them—the principal offers the new teacher support, and the teacher, in turn, makes a commitment to the school. However, in most cases, it is the district, not the school, that ultimately assumes responsibility for the teacher's employment. If a principal hires a mediocre or poor teacher without careful consideration and that teacher inadvertently receives tenure as a consequence of the principal's neglect and the passage of time, the district will be left with a long-standing tenure obligation. Therefore, central office administrators in Long Beach retained authority and responsibility for all hiring. Although principals in other districts might have objected if they could not make the job offer, Long Beach principals seemed to accept that arrangement and expressed overall satisfaction with the quality of the district's efforts and responsiveness to their preferences.

Layoffs and Reassignment—"Aye, there's the rub"

Even when principals have carefully chosen their teachers, they can't count on keeping them. That's true even if the teachers do a fine job in their position. For when budget cuts lead to program and staffing cuts, schools can lose prized teachers due to involuntary transfers or layoffs. Seniority usually determines which teacher will be laid off or moved to another school. Some teachers who are transferred are excellent, but others are not. In that case, the central office may require a school with an open position to accept a weak, but tenured, teacher who lacks an assignment. These "must place" teachers avoid the careful matching and commitment between a teacher and school staff that can be established during a thorough hiring process. Feeling powerless in the face of layoffs and reassignments, many principals we interviewed acted as zealous stakeholders, calculating and competing with their counterparts on behalf of their school.

Some principals had developed sophisticated tactics to avoid confrontations with the central office. When they anticipated losing key junior teachers, they might encourage them to earn a license in an additional field or two so that they could keep a position in their school. A Long Beach central administrator observed with some admiration how the principals "are so smart about that. They really are. One of the things they've learned over the years is credentialing, and they're the coaches to their employees. They didn't go into education to learn about employment law, but they have learned it."

We found that layoff decisions were largely based on seniority, due to state laws, the teachers' contracts, or local school board policy. Only charter schools in Baltimore were not bound by seniority-based layoffs. This last-in-first-out policy gives priority to teachers who have more experience and/or have achieved tenure in the district. An Aldine principal explained his dissatisfaction with the district's seniority-based layoff policy: "I wish [last-in-first-out] didn't have to be the rule, because some of your last-hireds are your best teachers, because they come in with fresh, new ideas. And we have those veteran teachers who are stuck in the Stone Age sometimes and don't want to change. So sometimes it's rough. I wish we could pick." Charlotte-Mecklenburg was unique in specifying that when positions were cut, teachers whose students had low test scores should be required to transfer (or be laid off, if they lacked seniority in the district). Although this approach might benefit students in an affected school, it created what one principal called "the [transfer] pool of everyone's worst," making it unlikely that any principal would voluntarily accept an excessed teacher who held tenure and had to be placed.

The process of excessing and reassigning teachers frustrated and demoralized some principals, although it energized others, who schemed to use the complicated rules to their school's advantage. One Montgomery County principal said, "Well, I love it. It's a big puzzle to me. I get very excited in March, and when it starts I find it fascinating how you put the pieces of that puzzle together. You strategize over those pieces, calculating where to make program cuts and when to conceal or post open positions." A Long Beach principal described how she protected a sixth grade class from an unwanted assignment by the district: "What I did is I moved that literacy person into the open sixth grade spot so [central office administrators] couldn't just place anyone there. And now I can interview [for the literacy position, which requires specialized qualifications]." Although this principal said, "I know everybody does it," some principals lacked the skills and savvy to manage the process well, and they sometimes ended up being dissatisfied with a forced placement.

Principals also complained about colleagues who failed to evaluate and dismiss poor probationary teachers before they received tenure, thus causing repeated transfers and forced placements—a process colloquially called "the dance of the lemons" or "passing the trash." A Montgomery County principal criticized colleagues who had not conducted serious evaluations that might lead to dismissals, saying, "They just play games and pass them on. [Over time,] one is going to be dropped in your lap, and you say, 'No, not going to happen.' Sometimes you win those and sometimes you still don't."

"It's All About Teachers. It's All About Teachers"

The principals and central office administrators in our study appeared to collaborate effectively in recruiting and hiring teachers, especially when the district had a strong capacity to recruit candidates widely, maintain a pipeline with the universities, and conduct an informative screening process. In all five districts, principals could engage school-based committees in making those decisions, and in four of the districts principals had the right to offer a job to a candidate.

However, layoffs and reassignment had the potential to pit the principals against the district as they calculated how to retain their best teachers, whatever their seniority, and how to avoid "must place" assignments made by the central office. Principals competed both among themselves and with the district office to secure the reassignment of teachers they wanted and to avoid those they dreaded. Those who could game the system by using the rules and timetable to their school's advantage emerged the winners. We found that centralized, standardized rules for layoffs and reassignments could work well when principals and central administrators accepted responsibility for regularly evaluating teachers, granting tenure judiciously, and moving to dismiss those who were ineffective. Often, however, principals or district officials fell short in this process, and ineffective teachers continued to lay claim to a position, much to the consternation of the receiving principal—and likely to the detriment of the teacher's students.

THE ACADEMIC PROGRAM IS INCREASINGLY IN THE DISTRICT'S CONTROL

Most analysts would argue that policy reforms in curriculum and assessment over the past decade have benefited low-income and minority students, long ignored or underserved by public schools. With the steady expansion of standardized curriculum, pedagogy, and assessments, as well as federal requirements that schools succeed with all subgroups of students, more students in urban districts are likely to have access today to a good education. However, the principals in these districts expressed concern about whether the requirements would allow time and provide support for creative, ambitious, challenging teaching in all schools.

Most of the administrators we interviewed accepted—whether whole-heartedly, with ambivalence, or grudgingly—standardized assessments as inevitable. Generally, they did not contest the district's right to choose a curriculum or even a basic pedagogy. This was especially true when central office administrators solicited feedback from those in the schools, as Long Beach did with its pilot programs and Montgomery County did by engaging teachers in curriculum development. However, they did object when the mandatory interim assessments were out of sync with the curriculum or the district required teachers to commit too much instructional time to interim testing or test preparation.

Some principals distinguished between curriculum that served as a floor, which creative teachers could then rise above, and curriculum that imposed a ceiling on what teachers could teach and their students could learn. This might happen if district administrators prescribed specific lessons that teachers had to follow—sometimes including scripts—or required teachers to submit to a detailed pacing guide specifying what they should teach each day. In those circumstances teachers were not permitted to move on to more complex topics if their students had mastered the basics, nor could they explore more inventive or demanding instructional approaches in order to promote students' creativity or develop their critical thinking skills. Central administrators in Long Beach, where common course outlines came complete with pacing guides, emphasized that the requirements were sufficiently general to allow teachers to do more. A principal concurred, saying, "There's tremendous backbone in this district around curriculum resources and curriculum maps, and things like that, that teachers don't have to make up. Nor is it suggested that they do make up their course material. So, there's definitely standardization as to what teachers can use. But I think our teachers would also tell you that they've had a lot of access to supplemental resources and to having a say in adding a layer on top of what's the standard curriculum." In Montgomery County, where interim assessments drove instructional pacing guides, principals widely reported that the district's curriculum—which was created and revised centrally with participation and advice from teachers—was ambitious and challenging for both teachers and students. A principal said that it "is much more rigorous than some of the state standards and really goes above and beyond . . . I'm blown away by how incredible [the curriculum] is and also how a teacher can enhance it, how a teacher can differentiate it, so it's not just a curriculum anymore. It's really how you use it."

In Charlotte-Mecklenburg, where elementary teachers were required to use the scripted literacy curriculum Open Court, two principals said that teachers could still enrich that basic curriculum. One observed, "If there are things that you want to embed, to kind of beef it up and up the rigor, you're able to do that." Another said, "It's been a major shift from four or five years ago [when we said], 'Hey, you'd better be on page such-and-such of the pacing guide when we come into your classroom,' to now, where the conversation is, 'You know that the curriculum, in and of itself, with our population, is not rigorous enough. We've got to do more. We've got to push. We've got to enrich. We've got to move forward.'" Still, schools were expected to make steady progress in test scores, as a district administrator explained: "It's not a gotcha. It's just . . . how we apply pressure and support."

Several Charlotte-Mecklenburg principals described how they nonetheless maintained some independence. One, who contended that the district's scope and sequence "doesn't make sense," said that his school would wait until the fourth quarter to teach what the curriculum called for them to teach during the first quarter: "So when we're testing on that the first quarter, my scores will be low because we haven't taught it. I've always had that understanding with the district office that I could do that."

SUMMARY

In all five districts we studied, principals functioned as stakeholders, advocating on behalf of their schools, pointing out problems caused by centralized policies or practices, jockeying to get the best available services, petitioning to protect their signature programs from cuts, or gaming the system to attract and retain the best possible teachers. Many we spoke with were informed, active, and influential throughout the process. As they maneuvered, calculated, or tried to hold their ground in a debate about what their school deserved, they sometimes annoyed central office administrators. However, to most district officials, these enterprising principals were a source of ongoing feedback and advice about how things were going in the schools and how they might be better. Without them, central administrators could mistakenly assume that seemingly even-handed solutions would suffice for all schools and communities, and, as a result, teachers might fail to exercise their best professional judgment.

Therefore, ensuring that principals can continue to play an active, informative, and constructive role in relation to the central office arguably strengthens a district's capacity to improve students' learning. This means that district officials have to appoint principals who have deep knowledge about instruction, strong analytic and managerial skills, persistence in pursuing what's possible, and, when warranted, a readiness to "talk truth to power." Some district leaders probably view these characteristics as antithetical to what they expect from principals. Yet having principals who can simultaneously serve as insiders and outsiders in the school system may be just what they need.

The principals we interviewed understood clearly that decisions about the size and allocation of the school's budget, the composition of its teaching staff, and the components of its academic program combined to determine their school's success. It's no surprise that they spoke forcefully, sometimes passionately, about retaining control of decisions they thought they were entitled to make. Given their intense interest, it was notable how often principals credited central administrators with having good intentions and providing welcome support and expertise. This appeared to be true even when the principals were not entirely satisfied with the influence they ultimately could exercise. Principals in various districts regretted—even resented—losing the right to say how fewer dollars could be spent. They objected to being required to accept a teacher on reassignment who should have been dismissed long ago. And they chafed when the district's benchmark assessments were out of sync with their best teachers' judgments about when and how topics should be taught. However, they were notably respectful of the challenges that district officials faced, forgiving them when things sometimes went awry and grateful for the support that they usually offered.

In part, principals pulled back from outright opposition because they basically trusted these central administrators. Each of these five districts had enjoyed a period of stable leadership and continuity districtwide—three for as long as a decade. Over that time, central and school leaders had developed an understanding that they shared an interest in the district's success and could count on each other's good intentions, even in challenging times. Intermediaries appointed by the district office often effectively served as advocates and brokers, moving easily back and forth between the schools and the central office. Because all these players were stakeholders in the context of state education policy, they were inclined to cooperate, if only out of shared self-interest. However, more often the alliance between principals and central administrators appeared to be grounded in long-term trust. Most principals in these districts respected central office administrators for their hard work, considered judgment, and fairness. This level of respect by principals for district administrators, and vice-versa, is not the norm in large urban districts and appears to be important in distinguishing these districts from many others that resemble them demographically.

LESSONS FOR PRACTICE

Some who read this account might conclude that central office administrators need not worry about principals' priorities and concerns, since the central office–schools relationships described here generally were respectful and amicable. However, that would be a mistake. The relationships we studied were neither inevitable nor accidental. Instead, central administrators in each of these districts had sought to develop and maintain a dynamic, constructive relationship between principals and central office administrators.

Based on our analysis of principals' relationships with their central office, we learned some important things about what worked, what might have worked better, and what practices others might replicate. We offer the following recommendations for district and school leaders:

⊃ *Appoint strong, skilled principals who can represent the interests of both their school and the district.* Compliant or unduly cautious school administrators will fail to inform the central office about the special strengths and needs of their school. At the same time, principals must be team players who recognize the needs of the district and respect their colleagues.

⊃ *Recognize the important role of trust in central office–schools relationships.* Difficult financial or political times can strain relationships between principals and central administrators. Trust that has been built gradually through respectful, consistent, and fair interactions makes it more likely that a school district and its schools will successfully weather such strains.

⊃ *Ensure that the district can respond to different levels of student need.* Within any large, urban district, the wealth and well-being of local schools and communities vary widely. When funds are cut, the differences between schools in wealthy and low-income communities are likely to be exacerbated—and, in response, the relationships between schools and the central office may become more strained. Therefore, district leaders should pay close attention to the apparent winners and losers as funding levels change, explaining to all their constituents why they have an interest in the more equitable distribution of funds. They should also encourage all principals to rely on one another to meet their school's needs. Although the process of distributing dollars may be a zero-sum game, the open exchange of expertise and ideas need not be.

⊃ *Allow at least some flexibility for principals in budgeting.* Although districts may not be able or willing to give principals full discretion over their budgets, they can provide at least some flexibility so that principals respond creatively to school-specific needs. Districts also should provide training or assistance in development of the budget to ensure that principals can effectively exercise that flexibility.

⊃ *Maintain an active and strong system for recruiting and screening teachers.* Although principals want to hire promising teachers who are well matched to their school's needs, most have neither the time nor the capacity to do this work well on their own. The resources of the central office should be committed to developing talent pipelines with local, state, and national preparation programs; screening candidates for basic qualifications; and providing processes that smoothly and quickly move desired candidates to become committed employees.

⊃ *Give principals and schools the right to select their teachers.* Although principals should not be expected to recruit new teachers on their own, they should be encouraged to choose those they hire. It is important to provide candidates with an informative hiring process that offers a good preview of work in the school. The principal and others involved in selection at the school must understand the expectations that a candidate may have for them. Even if principals are not permitted to make job offers, it should be clear to all involved that a teacher is hired because a school chose him or her.

⊃ *Monitor and support an effective evaluation and dismissal process.* The most contentious staffing problems occur when central administrators place weak, tenured teachers in positions contrary to the principal's best judgment. This would occur far less often if principals were required to evaluate teachers regularly and district officials would subsequently follow due process and move to dismiss failing teachers.

⊃ *Provide a solid curriculum and assessment system, but allow for school-based adaptation.* Most of the districts in this study had well-developed curricula and assessments. Some schools, however, chose to adapt the core curricula and adjust the interim assessments in response to teachers' judgment and students' needs. It is wise to allow the school to balance standardized expectations with accommodations that expert teachers deem effective in serving their students.

⊃ *Treat the academic program as the floor, not the ceiling, for perform-ance.* Increasingly, district leaders are raising concerns about the lack of rigor in their state's assessments. Principals, too, worry that standardized tests have "dumbed-down" instruction. Being forced to dedicate large amounts of time to reviewing basic material or preparing students for the mechanics of test taking will shortchange students and may lead parents with high academic expectations to take their children out of the system.

FIVE

Understanding the Power of Culture

When Peter Gorman took on the role of superintendent of Charlotte-Mecklenburg in 2006, the board of education gave him a mandate for change. As he explained,

> [The board] had adopted a theory of action that said, "We will decentralize." It says that in the theory of action. So, I thought, "Wow, I believe in that, so that lines up with my philosophical beliefs." It said that "we will differentiate resources for kids." Okay, I believe that. "We'll develop an accountability system." Okay, I believe that. It said that "we will focus on the HR side of the business and effective teachers." Okay, I believe that. So, contextually what happened was the board heard these things from the community, decided we're going to go this different direction, gave the basic, broad tenets, and the leadership team that we brought in inherited the theory of action where the board looked at us and said, "Okay, go do it."

Gorman saw this mandate to decentralize and shift the relationship between the central office and the schools as an exciting opportunity, but also one that had challenging implications for the organizational culture of the district. It called for new ways of managing and leading, new approaches to curriculum and instruction, and entirely new expectations for principals and how they would do their work. What the school board might have viewed as a straightforward change in management actually also called for a major shift in the district's culture, especially in how principals viewed and acted on their responsibilities and opportunities for leadership.

In advising Gorman, one keen observer explained the problem in terms of what he called "the free-range chicken concept": "You've got principals that have been penned up, and now you've opened the door to the pen because you're going to declare them free range, [but] they don't leave the pen. Well, why would you expect them to leave the pen if that's where they've been raised and that's what's been safe, and that's where they think the boundaries are?" Often, when leaders such as Gorman enter a district, they define a new strategy, with or without the board's prodding. Thoughtful leaders will realize that an effective strategy must be grounded in a practical, convincing theory of action. In moving forward, these leaders and those in their cabinet are likely to restructure roles, redesign systems, and reallocate resources. They may even redistribute decision rights for the strategic priorities so that principals gain more or less discretion over important matters that affect teaching and learning in their schools. And yet, as the chicken coop analogy suggests, those who must make the reforms work—including those closest to the classroom—are likely to feel bound by old norms, deep-seated values, and familiar habits. These elements of the culture they know best may actually interfere with initiatives that new leaders like Gorman champion, making it difficult to successfully institute change. Difficult, that is, but not impossible.

In this chapter, we explore the power of organizational culture and how it plays out in the interaction between the central office and the schools. Generally, culture is an overlooked ingredient in building a coherent system. Superintendents may take culture for granted or assume that it is fixed and immutable. Some find the challenge of changing the culture daunting and, therefore, not worth undertaking. Alternatively, they may assume that culture is inconsequential in the face of major strategic initiatives and not worth close attention. Or they may figure that cultural changes automatically flow from structural reforms and, therefore, don't warrant district leaders' focused attention. Sometimes district leaders acknowledge the presence of culture but then address it superficially—for example, by creating a new slogan or logo to convince employees and stakeholders that the district is different and has, in fact, adopted an "empowerment culture" or become committed to "shared professional responsibility."

Here we suggest something quite different. Based on our study, we argue that culture is a critical ingredient in any reform strategy. It is inextricably linked to the district's theory of change, strategy, organizational elements, and ongoing relationships between principals and district officials. Understanding the power of culture, where it comes from, and the context in which it is embedded can enable the effective implementation of good ideas. It can make the difference between a successful strategy and a failed one. Because organizational culture is fundamentally about the norms, behaviors, and values that guide how work gets done day to day in the district, it is key to successful performance. However, it is important to remember that culture also can present a significant barrier to change, and, if it is ignored or poorly understood, the organizational culture can set back a district's chances to improve students' learning.

We organize the discussion around three central questions often asked about culture and change. First, to set the stage, we respond to the question "What do you mean by organizational culture?" and explain the role that culture plays in developing an effective relationship between the central office and the schools. Second, we address the question "What does culture look like?" by depicting the experiences with culture of district leaders in our study. And third, we answer the question "How does culture work?" by dispelling three myths about culture and explaining why culture can, alternatively, block or facilitate change. Throughout, we draw on examples from the five districts we studied.

WHAT DO WE MEAN BY *CULTURE?*

There are many ways to think about culture, but here we refer to it as the set of prevailing norms and values expressed by individuals throughout the district. That is, in seeking to identify a district's culture, rather than taking for granted the behaviors and practices that central office administrators say *should* occur, we look at what people *actually do* and listen carefully as they explain what motivates their actions. In short, a district's organizational culture can be thought of as "the way things are done around here."[1]

The term *organizational culture* has its roots in the field of organizational behavior, which focuses on the human side of any organization or system of organizations. Originally, scholars became interested in the idea of culture when they noticed that organizational performance is often affected more by the norms that guide peoples' behavior than by the formal structure or organizational chart.[2] In 1982, Peters and Waterman popularized the notion of organizational culture in their book *In Search of Excellence.* Since then, the topic has received a good deal of attention, especially in management literature.[3] In their original 7-S management framework, for example, Peters and Waterman conceived of culture as "shared values" and placed it at the very center of their alignment framework.[4] When applied to public schooling, their model suggests that if administrators, teachers, and support staff share a set of values and norms that are coherent with the structure, systems, and strategies of the district, then the entire system has a better chance of improving the learning and performance of students.

Certainly, individual schools have their own culture, which may in turn influence the district's culture. But the unit of analysis in this study is the district, and so we focus on the norms and values that run throughout that organization. Expressions of culture are apparent in the kinds of things people actually say and do on their own. Therefore, culture is a reflection of the informal organization, not what is formally required or mandated by the district. For example, if the district expects principals to comply with certain policies but in actual practice they never do, then the shared norm would be to resist or ignore the district's mandates. Although most of the principals we interviewed suggested that such defiance was unusual in their district, some did describe situations where it occurred.

Although every organization has a culture, cultures can and do vary in strength. A culture is said to be "strong" when norms and values are pervasive and consistently shared by most people. In contrast, culture is said to be "weak" when norms and values are diffuse, and the behaviors they engender vary widely. Sometimes, organizational culture is contested when subgroups hold competing beliefs, norms, and values, which then lead them to act in different ways. For example, the principals and teachers in some schools may respect district directives and value compliance with them, while those in other schools may routinely dispute the wisdom or authority of central office administrators and ignore their expectations. In general, a district with a strong, positive, shared culture works better than one with either a weak and diffuse or a contested culture, because guiding people's behaviors and practices with norms is far more efficient and effective than imposing costly and annoying oversight. Further, a strong positive culture can enhance a district's capacity to effectively implement its strategy by promoting coherence both in carrying out organizational functions and gaining participants' ongoing investment and support.

However, strong cultures with coherent values and norms are not always beneficial because they may promote or condone unethical or misguided behavior. And although a strong, positive district culture can enhance opportunities to improve performance, it also may come with liabilities. Its very strength may lead participants to resist change as they hold tight to what they know and believe. Furthermore, changes in the environment may make some values and behaviors associated with a strong culture counterproductive as a district tries to meet the demands of new state or federal policies.

Just as we found no surefire strategy for all districts, we did not find a single approach to culture that was reliably successful. However, we did see that effective organizational cultures depend a great deal on the clarity of the values, beliefs, and behaviors expressed and expected by district officials.[5] With clear values and beliefs, prospective employees know what to expect and what the organization will reward if they join. Ultimately, what matters is the coherence between a district's culture and the implementation of its strategy.

Our study reminds us that district leaders can and should pay close attention to culture, both the one that exists and the one they hope to create, for culture can either reinforce or undermine changes that are under way. Indeed, district culture can play a special role in this process by increasing coherence and, in turn, enhancing the district's performance. Culture is an essential element for the effective implementation of strategic decisions and for their subsequent maintenance and sustainability. And given that culture is dynamic and deeply embedded in the fluid activities of the district, it can affect decisions made in the other parts of the system as well.

WHAT DOES DISTRICT CULTURE LOOK LIKE?

Each of the districts we studied had a unique organizational culture. Aldine and Long Beach had particularly strong cultures, where consistent evidence about norms, beliefs, and values echoed throughout our interviews with the central office administrators and principals. Over time, these districts had established ways of working that were grounded in explicit assumptions and values that were widely shared by employees at all levels. We discuss each district here to illustrate what we mean by a district's culture and to explain how that culture relates to central office–schools relationships.

Aldine

Those we interviewed in Aldine often referred to their strong, stable culture as "the Aldine Way." Superintendent Wanda Bamberg identified the basic norms of the Aldine Way as "work hard, don't complain, and do the right thing for kids." Others we interviewed emphasized the importance of working hard on behalf of students. Principals endorsed these values, although it became clear that it was the central office administrators who defined what the "right thing" was regarding curriculum, staffing, and, to a large extent, budgeting. The district culture also included the belief that administrators and teachers should be held accountable for producing "exemplary results" and granted more autonomy if and when they did. As one principal said, "The nonnegotiable culture of high expectations for students and staff" served as an enabling element that was sustained from the top. Another principal remarked, "We have high expectations for ourselves that carry over to the students. And so, if we have a staff member who is negative, they automatically don't fit in, because our teachers do whatever it takes for the kids to be successful. It's coming in early. It's staying late." An elementary school principal explained how high expectations and results related to autonomy for school leaders: "If you're getting exemplary ratings from the state, [then district administrators] are not on your case at all. How much do they help us? Our school is pretty much on its own because we're a high performer. We're high performing, and we're left alone." However, because the central office prescribed many details about how to achieve "exemplary results," consistency in practice remained quite strong. There seemed to be no cultural rewards for rebellion in Aldine.

The district's culture of hard work, commitment, and overall consistency supported its strategic priorities—academic programming, staffing, and budgeting. First, with the academic program, principals often mentioned the districts' loose-tight philosophy (loose on means and tight on ends). However, Aldine's emphasis on standardized curriculum and high-stakes testing suggested that endorsing the Aldine Way involved a substantial measure of compliance with the expectations of those in the central office, which were often communicated in subtle but persuasive ways. A principal suggested this in describing one district document that was widely circulated: "There's a score by my school, and my name is at the top of the list by the school. You know, they don't literally come out and say, 'You better perform.' They just say, 'We'd like you to be an exemplary school.' Who wouldn't, you know?" In these ways, Aldine's culture of working hard and focusing on the "right thing" facilitated the district's capacity to implement a consistent approach to academic programming; if principals were "not complaining" and believed in earned autonomy, then the district could, with little resistance, effectively execute what was essentially a centrally mandated academic program.

Aldine's culture was also well aligned with its policies and practices for staffing. Principals reported that they felt they had considerable flexibility to hire teachers. One said, "Central office pretty much lets you staff your own campus. [They] let you do what you wanted to do; I can actually say that. They tell you how many teachers you have and, based on what you need on your campus, you staff your campus based on your campus needs." At the same time, an assigned central office "staffing specialist" was highly involved in school-site hiring decisions, narrowing the list of those who could be interviewed and challenging whether candidates the principal preferred were truly qualified. Staffing decisions also were influenced by the lengthy tenure of most district employees and school board members. There was a strong tradition of hiring and promoting from within the district, both factors that rewarded loyalty and reinforced conservative aspects of the culture. All of this contributed to a felt sense of stability and consistency in Aldine, where beliefs about high commitment and hard work—all in keeping with central office expectations—paid off.

The district's strategic priority regarding budgeting was also generally well aligned with its expectations that principals would incline toward conformity. Schools had considerable freedom in deciding how to spend funds from the federal Title I and the Texas Compensatory Education Program. Several principals said that, although school leaders could "write our rationale" for their funding decisions, those decisions had to "be in line with the district goals" and "aligned with school-based improvement plans," which were reviewed by district officials. From the perspective of those in the central office, such oversight was necessary because some principals lacked budgeting skills. Therefore, in this aspect of school-based management, too, the principals' decision rights were circumscribed by a conservative culture that valued hard work, not complaining (particularly about central office mandates), and getting better student test results.

Although Aldine's strong culture enabled the district to make substantial progress in student achievement—as measured by the state tests—there seemed to be some drawbacks associated with its strong, largely compliant culture. First, the culture that rewarded loyalty also appeared to discourage rigorous review of personnel. We learned that very few principals ever lost their jobs. Indeed, one administrator reported that when principals did leave, they were often told to "identify and develop their [own] replacements." Such evidence suggests that the Aldine Way cultivates a rather insular culture. Although students had improved their performance on the state's test, the district's prescriptive approaches to curriculum, pedagogy, and assessment had made it difficult to achieve high levels of success when compared with similar districts in other states. It appeared that aspects of the Aldine Way might be limiting the district's readiness to critically review their practices and to make substantial changes.

Long Beach

The organizational culture in Long Beach was also strong but appeared to be more reciprocal and responsive to the expertise and views of those throughout the system than that of Aldine. The stability of the district over time and its very localized staffing practices, which drew prospective teachers primarily from California State University, Long Beach, established strong, long-term professional and personal relationships among those working in the district. The fact that principals and central administrators (including the superintendent) had spent considerable time acquiring and demonstrating skills as teachers and site administrators in Long Beach before being promoted to central office positions increased confidence throughout the district that they knew what they were doing. Therefore, professional trust and assurance in central administrators' knowledge, expertise, and good intentions ran high.

The district's approach to pilot testing new approaches before widely implementing them illustrates how this reciprocal, respectful culture supported efforts to improve the academic program. Whether a proposed change emanated from a school or a department in the central office, it was first introduced and developed in a limited setting where principals and teachers could try the program, review it, and refine it. Sometimes initiatives that were found wanting never moved beyond the pilot stage, but those that did were informed by the early experiences of those who piloted them. Once the district decided to adopt a program, it expected the principals and teachers to make it their own, both out of respect for central administrators and for their colleagues who had tested and improved it. A principal summarized: "Rarely is anything introduced as a program you have to do. [Central office administrators] say, 'We're offering it.' Then, eventually, it becomes, 'Okay. We're going to do it districtwide.'"

At the time of our study, the culture of Long Beach appeared to be largely in line with its strategic priorities. For example, that the majority of budgeting decisions were made by central office seemed to be supported by the cultural norm of respecting the expertise of central administrators and abiding by their decisions. This was particularly notable as principals acquiesced to Superintendent Steinhauser's decision to consolidate all Title I funds centrally rather than continue to distribute them to principals, who could decide how to spend their school's share. Although some principals disagreed with this decision, they still acknowledged that it was well-intentioned and consistent with a districtwide commitment to what one called "equity and access for everyone." Indeed, we argue that it was precisely because of the district's strong relational, reciprocal culture that principals were inclined to trust Steinhauser's judgment. Principals might have objected to this decision as countercultural because those in the central office did not pilot test its effects; yet, the principals' response was consistent with a Long Beach culture that featured mutual trust and shared responsibility among all its educators as they sought to do the best with what they had on behalf of students.

Similarly, in developing their academic program, teachers expressed their views through focus groups and surveys. Ultimately, however, the content standards, targeted interventions, and assessments were standardized across the district. The central office provided the schools with tools for linking the common assessments, content standards, and pacing guides, all of which were intended to support teachers and their students in reaching district standards. Again, the district's use of focus groups and pilot projects in advance of district-mandated implementation is evidence of an organizational culture that values consultation with those in schools and classrooms.

Staffing and hiring practices, which Long Beach carried out according to established rules and procedures, also reflected a commitment to a widespread norm of shared responsibility. This was the only district we studied where principals could not make job offers to teaching candidates, though they seemed unbothered by their lack of formal authority for hiring and, instead, seemed confident not only that the process conducted by central administrators would be thorough and efficient but also that their own preferences would be respected. One principal explained that the centralized hiring process was necessary "to make sure that there's equity across the district." Further, the fact that the teachers union reportedly never "protested a dismissal" while the administration never deviated from seniority in layoffs illustrated the reciprocal, relational aspects of the culture.

In sum, the district's approach to these strategic priorities of budgeting, academic programming, and staffing contributed to and reinforced norms of respect and relational accountability, which were central to the organizational culture in Long Beach.

HOW DOES CULTURE AFFECT CHANGE?

In the midst of major efforts to reform how an organization functions, people often hold on to their beliefs about culture, which can make it difficult to change practice in meaningful ways. We draw on evidence from our study to refute three very different myths about the role that organizational culture plays in district leaders' efforts to implement their strategy. Some district officials proceed as if culture is peripheral to the change process. Others assume that changing culture is relatively straightforward, requiring little attention. And still others act as if culture is not amenable to change. However, as we will show, district culture does matter and can indeed be changed, although this is no simple matter. Nevertheless, culture cannot be ignored when implementing a strategy, since changes in policy and culture should go hand in hand.

Myth 1: Culture Is Peripheral to the Change Process

Those intent on improving a school district often believe that culture is peripheral to the change process. Compared with the clear and consequential improvements that seem possible as a result of creating new structures, redesigning systems, and reallocating resources, culture can appear to be amorphous and somewhat irrelevant. However, years of research in other sectors, including health care, suggest otherwise.[6] Indeed, recent research shows that school culture, as reported by teachers, is critical to the kinds of improvements in learning and achievement that a district can accomplish.[7] In our research, too, we found ample evidence that culture plays an important role in efforts to improve a district, both in what is possible to accomplish and what is difficult to change.

Consider, for example, the case of Montgomery County. At the time of our interviews, the district was in the first year of its transition from a decade of leadership by Jerry Weast to the administration of Josh Starr. When Starr entered the district, he found a very strong culture of high expectations and accountability, a culture that actually shaped the kinds of changes that he chose to initiate.

Under Weast, the district had made significant progress in achieving equity and access for the wide range of students who attended Montgomery County schools.[8] It had developed a strong culture of accountability that was focused on equity and driven by results. A deliberate reallocation of resources from schools located in wealthy communities to schools in low-income communities demonstrated this commitment to equity. Over time, higher performance by students in these targeted, low-income schools paid off, demonstrating the benefits of focusing resources, appointing principals who were strong leaders, and closely monitoring students' progress in all schools. People generally believed in this formula for improvement, in part because of the strong partnership that Weast developed between the district officials and the principals. His commitment to shared governance had given teachers and principals both real and influential seats at the decision-making table. Through that structure, the culture of shared responsibility grew as employees from all groups came to understand their part in improving students' performance and took pride when the programs they enacted paid off.

When we conducted our interviews, Starr and several of the principals suggested that some aspects of this culture discouraged principals from speaking up and questioning the district's accountability practices, especially in meetings attended by central office admin-istrators. In their view, the district was not, in scholar Edmonson's terms, "psychologically safe."[9] According to one elementary school principal, "when Dr. Weast was here, the culture was top-down, more intense. You basically were on call twenty-four hours a day."

On stepping into his new role, Starr aimed to change the district's culture. He planned to remove the threat that he perceived some administrators felt while also reinforcing the district's well-established commitment to equity, shared governance, fairness, and transpar-ency. Starr explained that the district had been "a results-driven, out-comes-driven organization, where you live and die by your test scores." He had heard that the culture created "a degree of fear" among peo-ple who had learned to "toe the line, do what you're told, don't ask too many questions." He said, "We're going to continue to build this cul-ture here where people are focused on our values and we're united in that work . . . [but] try to break down some of the [barriers].

The cultural changes that Starr intended to make were most closely related to the assessment component of the academic program. He thought that when district administrators visited a school and scrutinized student test data, they sometimes generated undue anx-iety among teachers and principals, anxiety that could instill defen-sive responses and stall further improvement. Intending to reduce the principals' intensely felt sense of accountability for students' test scores, Starr hoped to change the culture by changing the role of the community superintendent and some of the systems within Mont-gomery County. Whether or not his new approach to the academic program and related strategic priorities will transform the district culture without undermining performance remains to be seen. What is clear, however, is that culture was central in the accomplishments under Weast's leadership and that it was central in Starr's assessment of what had to change if Montgomery County's schools were to sus-tain their record of improvement.

Myth 2: Changing Culture Is Relatively Straightforward

A second myth is that changing culture is relatively straightfor-ward. Leaders sometimes attempt to transform the culture of their organization by proclaiming the change itself by creating clever tag lines and branding or by distributing glossy materials that feature symbolic photos or logos. These activities essentially are attempts to announce that a new culture has arrived and, thus, make it so. Although symbols are often helpful in conveying aspirations and intentions, cultural change is rarely achieved directly or immediately.

As we saw in Josh Starr's approach to changing culture in Montgomery County, the culture of the existing system needs to be carefully considered. When he entered Montgomery County, it was evident to Starr that his success in implementing new initiatives was affected by the strong culture and legacy that Weast had built. As that illustration shows, if one views culture as "out there"—that is, something that is not inextricably linked to district priorities—it is easy to fall prey to this myth. We argue that it is critical to see culture as being central to a district's efforts to improve; if it is not, meaningful change is not likely to occur. However, when values and norms are deeply embedded in the district's current practices, it will be difficult to change that culture, unilaterally or by proclamation.

We learned another interesting lesson about changing culture in Charlotte-Mecklenburg, where attempts to formalize and reward elements of what had been the informal culture backfired, unintentionally bolstering norms and behaviors that were problematic. The norms that define a district's culture are actual behaviors and real beliefs, not what an entity such as the central office says they should be. Sometimes, as in Aldine and Long Beach, how principals think they should behave, given "the way things are done here," aligns with the expectations of those in the central office. However, sometimes that's not the case. In Charlotte-Mecklenburg, our interviews with principals suggested that they held the following cultural norms: despite what the district tells you about following appropriate procedures, you'll be more successful if you rely on your relationships with others in the district to cut deals and trade favors and get what you want; you should "fly under the radar" and, if necessary, rebel to get good work done; you should negotiate—indeed, you *must* negotiate in order to survive and succeed; and if your school performs well on state tests, you'll be rewarded.

When Gorman stepped in as superintendent, Charlotte-Mecklenburg's culture had been shaped by the district's history of close monitoring, managed instruction, and compliance with central office mandates. When the school board pushed for greater decentralization and school-based autonomy, emboldened principals aimed to gain more control in a system that historically had been top-down and tight. In the past, principals who resisted centralized control had done so somewhat furtively. A number of those we interviewed described how they had seized autonomy by working outside the formal rules of the system, by "flying under the radar." Recognizing the "free-range chicken" problem he faced, Gorman introduced several early initiatives meant to formalize this informal culture, to encourage and reward the innovation and quiet rebelliousness of principals.

> One of the things we've discovered is we've not done a good enough job with showing and making heroes out of those folks who are being autonomous in positive ways. As a matter of fact, there was almost an undercurrent that you like being a rebel. One successful principal called me and said, "I'm just so sorry about those things I said in the paper." I said, "Everything you said in the paper was great." She said, "Yeah, but if you go through the list of nonnegotiables, I essentially said, 'I'm not doing that, I'm not doing that, I'm not doing that.'" We had this class of individuals who liked being the rebel. [They thought] it was better to be the one thumbing your nose at the district office. So, how do we then make heroes out of those folks publicly instead of letting them be heroes for going against what the district office says?

Many principals preferred tried-and-true modes of getting what they wanted by relying on their informal networks and work-arounds within the system. Two initiatives under Gorman, Strategic Staffing and Freedom and Flexibility, were explicit attempts to establish systems and structures that formally authorized principals to have flexibility and exercise autonomy in their work. However, in some cases, state laws and regulations still constrained what they could do. For example, because North Carolina funded local districts in staffing units rather than dollars, principals felt they had little freedom in managing their school budgets. Therefore, despite changes at the district level, principals still strongly valued and relied on their personal networks to get their good work done. Some followed the new guidelines, but many resorted to old norms and practices. Those who preferred functioning as "renegades" remained more interested in their own school's performance than in the success of the district. The result was a weak district culture with conflicting norms and a wide range of practices, some of them dysfunctional from the perspective of the district.

Although there had been clear efforts by central administrators to bring about "big cultural change" in Charlotte-Mecklenburg, often these initiatives encountered skepticism and resistance because of a strong culture that celebrated the renegades. As long as prevailing norms endorsed and encouraged rebelliousness, principals—particularly those seen as the stars in the system—found ways to continue doing things their way. Interestingly, the changes that Charlotte-Mecklenburg officials made to move decision-making authority out to the schools had been difficult to implement, in part because principals already exercised such authority outside the formal system. As this example suggests, when the district culture is strong, changing it can be extremely difficult.

Myth 3: Culture Cannot Be Changed

We've painted a picture of district culture that may be resistant to change if it is strong. However, it is also true that when elements of the academic program, staffing, and budgeting are carefully aligned with, or responsive to, the district culture, they can be used as levers for change. If a district is intentional about making strategic choices, then the current culture of the district can support the intended changes, and in the process the culture itself can be modified to achieve greater coherence with new programs and practices. Here, we consider the case of Baltimore City Public Schools and the changes that Andrés Alonso undertook when he became CEO there.

At the time of our visit to Baltimore, Alonso had been CEO for four years, having been appointed from outside based on his successful work as an administrator in New York City. Following months of meetings with local educators and community members, he introduced far-reaching programmatic and policy changes. One of the most notable was Bounded Autonomy, a program granting principals the right to make many important decisions about their school's academic program, budget, and staffing. This shift in authority ran counter to the well-established top-down culture of the district that preceded his appointment. The move to decentralize decisions was grounded in Alonso's belief that schools should be the key unit of change in a district's improvement strategy and that principals needed to tailor their budget, staff, and academic program to meet the needs of their students. However, just as Alonso believed that schools should not be constrained by unnecessary rules, he thought they also should not move ahead without "guidance." Therefore, the central office began to provide common standards, systems of accountability, guidance, and support to enable schools to improve learning for all Baltimore students.

The culture that Alonso first encountered in Baltimore was top-down and weak. Central office administrators told principals what to do, but compliance was uneven and school-based practices varied depending on the administration and teaching staff of each school. Some principals did their best to cope with the largely incoherent and unskilled central office staff by relying on relationships and favors to get what they needed. Unlike Charlotte-Mecklenburg, however, renegade principals did not enjoy cultural celebrity.

In an effort to rely more on the school-based knowledge and expertise of principals and teachers, Alonso dramatically reduced the size of the central office by letting go of administrators and staff whose jobs or performance were not contributing to effective school-based practices. This dramatic move sent a powerful message to principals that business as usual was over in Baltimore. Not only would central office administrators no longer have the authority to control principals' work, the principals themselves would be expected to step up and take responsibility for what happened in their school's classrooms and corridors. No longer able to blame or defer to central office administrators, they would have to assess their school's needs, manage its resources, hire and assign staff, and institute changes in the academic program that would increase students' learning. Each decision conveyed new norms about how leadership could and should be exercised.

When Alonso entered, he sought to find and support principals who were "problem solvers"—those who could be thoughtful contributors to the system as a whole. Over time, he also dismissed principals whose unproductive laissez-faire approach to management had led to dysfunctional, low performing schools. However, those principals who stayed said they appreciated having more control over key decisions. The changes in structures and systems that constituted the shift to bounded autonomy encouraged initiative and self-reliance. Yet, the new system did not simply grant full license to principals. Instead, district officials issued binders of guidelines explaining how principals could and should exercise their newfound autonomy. Over time, particularly after Alonso hired a chief academic officer with deep knowledge about literacy, the district's "guidance" about instruction became more explicit. However, respect for the CAO's expertise led principals to seriously consider and often accept her recommendations for assessment and professional development.

At the same time, Alonso's introduction of Fair Student Funding changed the distribution of resources in the district based on the student body demographic within the schools. The title drew attention to the new norm of fairness and conveyed his determination to serve all students well. Therefore, the new norms and values embedded in Alonso's policies and practices not only endorsed school-based autonomy but also signaled the importance of districtwide responsibility for equity.

To further support principals as they assumed their new responsibilities, district officials created sixteen school networks, each linked with a team of central administrators skilled in specific functions, such as budgeting, staffing, and curriculum. This new structure conveyed the clear message that the central office would be committed to hands-on support rather than command and control from afar. While the superintendent guided the rapidly emerging culture in the district, each change he made conveyed new messages about organizational values and priorities.

Overall, these changes in policy and practice led to a new, emerging organizational culture that valued initiative, school-based sufficiency, and districtwide responsibility. The clear message conveyed by these changes was that principals could invest in and take ownership of their school because of the system, not in spite of it. They were expected to be both strong managers and instructional leaders. Their work changed as a result of Bounded Autonomy and Fair Student Funding, but so did the cultural values and norms that guided that work.

In this new culture, those working in and for the Baltimore City Schools increasingly chose to exercise collective responsibility in order to improve student achievement and learning districtwide. This did not happen quickly or accidentally but was reinforced by informed, thoughtful decisions by Alonso and his team, along with principals and teacher leaders who increasingly shared responsibility for improving students' experience and accomplishments. The culture they were developing as a result of these changes had the potential to support longer-term goals for improving and sustaining the system as a whole.

SUMMARY

Culture is a critical element in any district's strategy for improvement. It is not the only factor that affects performance, but it can be very influential, either intentionally or unintentionally, for it has the potential to block, stall, or enhance implementation of reform. It is a kind of secret weapon that often goes unnoticed and certainly has been unappreciated and underutilized. Therefore, culture warrants special attention by those who seek to improve or fundamentally change how the district develops and manages its central office–schools relationships.[10]

Culture conveys what is truly valued, expected, allowed, and rewarded. Importantly, culture shapes what people actually do in their work. And yet culture cannot be dictated, demanded, or announced. Slick slogans that promise a lot but deliver little are unlikely to influence how administrators or teachers do their work. However, changes in policy and practice that are intentionally implemented affect the meaning that people make of the changes under way. Ultimately, that meaning is what matters in defining how principals and teachers carry out their work day to day in schools and classrooms.

Fortunately, culture is not as elusive or mysterious as administrators may believe. In fact, culture develops in response to what actually happens in the district. It emerges from the daily experiences of individuals as they encounter their district's approach to managing the key strategic priorities of budgeting, staffing, and the academic program. Changes in the structures, systems, and distribution of resources, which have consequences for these strategic priorities, affect and are affected by district culture. Thus, culture is not an amorphous concept that is somehow "out there" and beyond reach; in fact, culture is "in here." It is embedded in and expressed through the decisions, choices, responses, and interactions of central office and school-based personnel.

It's no secret that many initiatives or changes in practice may not actually work to produce their intended effects because these strategic choices are never implemented in a vacuum. The context, including the culture in which these decisions are made and implemented, will, through deliberate efforts or unwitting actions, affect a district's strategic reform agenda. Culture, therefore, deserves close attention.

LESSONS FOR PRACTICE

With these conclusions in mind, we offer the following lessons for practice:

- *Before implementing any reform initiative or change strategy, take time to understand the culture of your district.* Listen to what people say about how things really work. Observe the patterns of behavior that suggest what other administrators, principals, and teachers do and how they behave—not what you or your associates might say about the way it's supposed to be. These are not the "shoulds" mandated by the central office but the "shoulds" held close by those who work daily with the students and families of the district. For example, do principals respond well to tight expectations and guidelines from central office (as we found in Aldine), or do they rely on idiosyncratic solutions grounded in personal relationships (as we found in Charlotte-Mecklenburg)? Informal patterns of behavior, fueled by the existing culture, can be far more powerful than rules and regulations. Therefore, it makes sense to understand the culture that you have inherited.

- *Do not underestimate the power of culture.* Culture is an overlooked and yet critical ingredient to any change strategy. It both affects and is affected by the strategic priorities or reform strategy. As we saw in all the districts we studied, culture will influence how the systems and structures actually function (or fail to function), and, reciprocally, culture can be transformed as principals and teachers encounter and make sense of the new initiatives, policies, and practices. Therefore, rather than assuming that culture will take care of itself or that it doesn't matter, be intentional and thoughtful about the role that culture might play.

- *Recognize the pros and cons of strong, high-commitment cultures.* Although high-commitment cultures can certainly yield positive benefits when values and norms are widely shared, they also can make it difficult for a district to change. In Aldine we found a strong culture of high commitment, which made it difficult for the district to change in the face of new, more demanding state assessments. More generally, keep in mind that people can become accustomed to certain practices and patterns of behavior over time. These patterns can be efficient as well as effective in sustaining a high-commitment culture, but they can also reinforce insular views and henceforth, support resistance to change.

⊃ *You can choose the kind of culture you want your district to have, but you can't dictate it and expect to see results.* Declaring a new strategy or theory of change is possible, but you can't declare what a culture will be. Don't expect shiny PR pamphlets and other marketing tools to do the job when it comes to changing culture, for culture results from responses to the other decisions you make. It can't be mandated, no matter how pretty the messaging.

⊃ *You can change culture.* As we learned from Andrés Alonso's work in Baltimore, it's possible to change systems, structures, and the use of resources in ways that gradually strengthen the district's culture to support its strategy.

SIX

Navigating
the External
Environment

Managing the relationship between the central office and the schools is hard, often uncertain work. Baltimore CEO Alonso characterized the process as "stumbling toward coherence." He was not suggesting that a superintendent can inadvertently achieve success but, rather, that the work of district management and leadership is uncertain and ongoing. However, any superintendent who pursues serious change inevitably stumbles, in part because the external environment of the district is so complex and dynamic.

We have explored what it takes to achieve practical coherence among the many moving parts *within* the school district—the theory of change, strategy, organizational elements, culture, and the strategic priorities. However, we have not addressed the role of the external environment, which unexpectedly foils so many thoughtful and well-meaning district leaders as they try to implement and then sustain an effective and coherent strategy to improve learning. The district's external environment encompasses a wide range of economic, legal, political, social, and cultural factors and forces, most of which lie well beyond the reach of district leaders and often have an extraordinary, unforeseen impact on deliberate efforts to improve learning for all students.

In this chapter we highlight major factors in the external environment that all the superintendents in our study encountered as they designed and implemented their strategies for managing the central office–schools relationship. These factors sometimes aligned nicely to support deliberate change, but they also disrupted or diverted plans that otherwise appeared well-informed and reasonable. Although a superintendent may have little control over the forces that shape the district's external environment, this does not mean that they can safely be ignored, either initially or during the course of a district leader's tenure. By understanding the factors and forces of the environment and how they affect local educational policy and practice, district leaders can anticipate and deftly adjust to the many pressures and demands.

The environment is ever changing; what works at the start of an administration may not work at all a year later. It is never so simple as setting up a strategy under an initial set of conditions and letting it run. During periods of dynamic change—sudden changes in the financial markets, new federal and state laws, dramatic shifts in public opinion—districts may have to respond rapidly and substantially or be left with an increasingly incoherent strategy that has a deteriorated effect. Therefore, district leaders must monitor the environment both initially and over time in order to ensure that their theory of change, strategy, and consequent actions achieve their intended purpose.

We begin by identifying and describing the economic, legal, and political forces that shaped the districts' plans and practices for managing central office–schools relationships. Then we provide a more detailed account of how complex social and cultural forces, including experiences with the dynamics of race and social class, affected the districts' strategies in two districts—Charlotte-Mecklenburg and Montgomery County.

IT'S THE ECONOMY

Funding, among the most contentious challenges that public school officials face, is largely controlled by external forces. Funding includes revenue available to the district from many public and private local, state, and federal sources. Often, continuity of these funds is inseparable from the health of the broader economy. When that continuity is disrupted and budgets must be cut, it's the teachers and principals who experience the effects most directly.

As discussed in chapter 4, unexpected changes in funding provoked angry responses from principals in this study, who otherwise reported being satisfied that central office administrators took the schools' needs into account. The 2007–2008 global recession severely affected the funding of all five districts we studied, and those effects lingered and reverberated when we visited four years later. Local attempts to raise additional tax revenues for education encountered resistance or outright opposition, while decreases in state and/or local funding forced sudden budget cuts in nearly all of the districts.

Aldine was one of the hardest hit. Because over 90 percent of its students qualify for a free or reduced-priced lunch, Aldine had relied heavily on additional state and federal dollars to meet its students' needs. In the years following the recession of 2007–2008, Aldine lost nearly all of its state impact aid for low-income students. For example, in the 2006–2007 school year, Aldine was able to hire 396 teachers with the state impact aid.[1] By 2010–2011 that number had been cut to 89 districtwide, a loss of more than 300 teaching positions.[2] Some schools experienced budget cuts of hundreds of thousands of dollars once used to hire additional teachers and support staff. Notably, just months before the economy collapsed, Aldine's finances had not looked dire. In early 2007, voters approved a $365 million bond package to build twelve new schools over the following decade.[3] However, within just two years, the onset of the recession and the defeat of a proposal to raise additional local tax revenue for education forced district leaders to freeze wages, increase class sizes, and scale back reform efforts.[4] We see in Aldine how suddenly the economic environment can change, halt progress, and force the district to respond.

Charlotte-Mecklenburg was also severely affected by economic forces beyond its control. As a major U.S. financial center (home of Bank of America and Wachovia), Charlotte was hard hit by the collapse of the economy. With more than a quarter of the district's annual budget funded by county sources, the economic losses cut deeply into the district's resources. In the 2009–2010 school year alone, the district lost $34 million in funding from the county.[5] Facing the need to make large budget cuts, district leaders decided to close schools—many of which served high percentages of African American students—a move that undermined the goodwill that Superintendent Gorman had worked so hard to build with community members and parents.

When federal officials announced the Race to the Top (RTTT) competition, another dramatic change in the environment, state and district leaders had to decide how to respond. RTTT offered the chance to moderate the effects of funding cuts, but it came with substantial obligations. States and districts responded differently to those demands, and, as a result, only some districts benefited from the financial respite RTTT offered. For example, after Maryland was a winner in the first round of RTTT in 2010, Baltimore received more than $52 million, which became very important in funding Alonso's initiatives. However, Montgomery County (also located in Maryland) was entitled to $12 million from RTTT but received none because Superintendent Jerry Weast chose not to accede to RTTT's requirements to revamp its teacher evaluation system, arguing that the district's current professional growth system worked effectively.[6] North Carolina, a winner in the second round of RTTT funding, received about $400 million, and allocated just over $15 million to Charlotte-Mecklenburg. Texas never applied to RTTT, so Aldine did not have a chance at the money. California was a finalist twice but never won, and so Long Beach never received financial relief from the competition.

The dramatic changes in federal, state, and local funding following the recession illustrate how sudden, severe changes in the financial environment of school districts can wreak havoc on both current and proposed programs. However, the districts' varied experiences with RTTT demonstrate the impotence of district leaders in the face of state officials' decisions, as well as their potential to retain control of their priorities in the face of attractive funding opportunities.

IT'S THE LAW

Legal forces may be one of the most obvious environmental factors affecting school districts, but the ways in which they do so are not always clear. Legal forces include state and federal education statutes, regulations issued by the state department of education, and contract law. Repeatedly, district leaders explained how these legal forces affected what they could do to manage central office–schools relationships and how they could do it. The prominence of accountability policies and their effects on the academic program provide a far-reaching example.

In Aldine, state education policy affected the district's relationship to its schools' academic programming. The values and norms of the Aldine Way guided the relationship between the central office and the schools. However, over many years Texas education laws and regulations required that all districts administer a battery of state tests to ensure accountability for public education. The content of those tests and the prominence they played in state policy deeply affected Aldine's expectations for student learning and, thus, the schools' control of decisions about its academic program.

In 1979, Texas instituted a statewide testing program that, through periodic changes in legislation and policy, evolved in size, scope, and rigor.[7] From the 1980 Texas Assessment of Basic Skills (TABS) to the most recent State of Texas Assessments of Academic Readiness (STARR), the state has deliberately used standardized test results to measure student learning, publicize results, and thus take failing districts to task. Aldine's administrators realized that achieving recognition as a high performing district necessarily meant scoring well on the current Texas assessment. The district's prominent, well-established culture of high expectations and performance was unquestionably situated in and influenced by the testing requirements of the Texas regulatory environment. District officials deliberately aligned their decisions about academic programming, budgeting, and staffing with the expectations about performance created by the state test. The district maintained a prescriptive curriculum aligned with the Texas

Assessment of Knowledge and Skills (TAKS), which was being used at the time of our visit. The curriculum included detailed, six-week scope-and-sequence guides along with benchmark targets that specified what a student should know and be able to do. Each target was linked directly to a state standard assessed on the state test.

When we asked why Aldine did not also rely on other measures of performance, such as graduation rates and student performance on the SAT and ACT, a deputy superintendent explained that the district was too busy preparing students for the high-stakes test: "It's because of the force of the state. That's all we had time to do. We've tried to enhance TAKS, but you can only do so much when you've got exam after exam, test after test after test that's staring you in the face down the road." Aldine, therefore, adapted to the external testing environment, intent on serving students, achieving proficiency, and gaining credibility and respect statewide. The district's identity and its strategic decisions were tightly aligned with and shaped by the state requirements for student testing. All districts in our sample were subject to federal and state accountability policies, the standardized tests those policies required, and the media's subsequent publication of their results. Unlike the RTTT competition, local officials could not opt out. However, they could and did choose how to respond, and not all districts complied as vigorously as Aldine. Others, such as Baltimore, Montgomery, and Long Beach, ensured that standardized tests were not the only measure of the schools' success that they sought to improve. Meanwhile, many other legal forces—licensing requirements for teachers and principals, standards for learning time, the rights or prohibitions in state labor laws—influenced the form and details of central office–schools relationships.

IT'S POLITICS

The political forces a district might encounter in its environment include local school board dynamics and policies, the influence of special interest groups, politically motivated media accounts, debates about issues such as choice and accountability, and electoral politics at the local, state, and federal levels. In these five districts we saw how the political force of the school board affected coherence and the central office–schools relationship.

In Baltimore, Alonso reported to a ten-member board that was jointly appointed by the city's mayor and the governor of Maryland. The board reportedly gave Alonso "extremely wide berth" to "stir it up" when it hired him as superintendent in 2007.[8] One member even jokingly referred to Alonso as "Bulldozer Andrés" because of the sweeping changes they expected him to make.[9] Membership on the board was ultimately determined by the political battles for the two high-profile positions of mayor and governor. Board support for Alonso could have dissipated in the next mayoral or gubernatorial election. That Alonso was the seventh superintendent in ten years provided a strong reminder of how external politics could shape the fate of the school district.

In contrast to the dynamic, unpredictable role of the school board in Baltimore, the role of Aldine's school board was stable and predictable. When we visited in 2011, no member had fewer than five years' experience on the board, and two had served for more than twenty years. Members intending to leave the board—those retiring or not running for reelection—were encouraged to resign midterm, when the remaining members could appoint an interim replacement, who would then gain recognition and experience prior to the next election. In 2011, six of the seven members on the board had begun their service as appointees; no appointed member had lost a subsequent election in fifty years.[10]

The uncertain dynamic between the board and district in Baltimore contrasted sharply with the predictable, stable relationships in Aldine. Those of other districts fell between these extremes. But even in districts with conventional board elections, a one-vote change in the majority could mean abrupt dismissal of the superintendent and the programs he championed. As we saw in Charlotte-Mecklenburg, the school board issued a new mandate to decentralize the relationship between the central office and the schools. This aligned well with Gorman's priorities. However, when Gorman's comments endorsing merit pay for teachers generated conflict some years later, he, too, encountered the effects of the political environment.

IT'S SOCIAL AND CULTURAL

Social and cultural forces—such as historical legacies, public reputation and perceptions, and dynamics of race and class—have a complex and powerful impact on the relationship between the central office and the schools. Such forces shaped the prospects for coherence in all of these districts, but here we focus on three of the most compelling. Baltimore's national reputation and expectations about the school district strongly affected the central office and its ability to maintain productive relationships with schools. District leaders managed to confront and transform those perceptions by partnering with the community and enhancing the role of parents in local school decisions. In Charlotte-Mecklenburg and Montgomery County we saw how the legacy and history of race and class dynamics exerted pressure on the strategic direction of the district and the interactions among the central office, the schools, and the local communities.

Beliefs about Baltimore's Stagnate Progress in the Schools

The performance expectations and the culture of the Baltimore City Schools were strongly influenced by the district's negative reputation. Deeply rooted beliefs about the limits of what educators could accomplish in Baltimore threatened to stymie Andrés Alonso's goals and plans. The district had suffered from decades of decline and poor performance and was widely considered by members of the local community and the state government to be dysfunctional and failing. These views were further fueled by the negative portrayal of the city and its schools on the popular TV series *The Wire*. One Baltimore school leader said that the word *failure* had become attached to the district's name: "FBCPS—the Failing Baltimore City Public Schools." This central office administrator explained, "Before, when I was [working] in . . . other counties, people were like, 'The folks from Baltimore City? Why are you talking to them? I mean, they're incompetent, right?'"

These external perceptions were reflected in the internal culture and played out in the relationship between the central office and the schools. Principals struggled with what they saw as longtime endorsement of low expectations by central office administrators. The external environment's view of Baltimore's schools seemed to have been adopted by the district's top administrators. One principal recalled, "People would always say I had a good school, and really what that meant was we had a middle school population that wasn't killing anybody." Another remembered calling the central finance office to clean up errors in a data report: "The lady just chuckled and said, 'Yeah, things like that happen. Don't worry about it. You're not as bad as some other schools I have.' So basically, not being perfect, just being okay, was good."[11]

Low expectations, which prevailed in both the external environment and the internal culture, contributed to callous tolerance of students' poor performance and high dropout rates. The state's lack of confidence in, or hope for, the district's improvement yielded little external support for innovation and creativity. Without new approaches to academic programming, budgeting, and staffing, the district seemed stuck in a downward spiral of diminishing expectations and continuous failure.

When he became superintendent, Alonso was acutely aware of the challenge he faced to improve the schools given this negative reputation. However, his actions and strategies during his first year on the job seemed designed to disrupt beliefs and to transform the district's poor reputation rather than adapt to it. During his first two months, his staff coordinated five community meetings, strategically located throughout the district, where Alonso listened intently to parents' and community members' concerns and frustrations about the district.

He acknowledged that there was some discomfort among staff and stakeholders with his initial approach of engaging in so much community dialogue before presenting a vision and strategic plan for the district. "For the first month, people kept waiting for my blueprint," he recalled. "I refused to give them one." Instead, he said, "I went to five citywide community meetings where parents vented. They said, 'Central office is too big. We don't get the support, and schools don't listen to us.' I listened for a month and a half." One community member recalled how "there wasn't a 'here's where we're going' document until March 2008. There was a tremendous amount of conversation, a tremendous amount of listening, and then there was this constant drumbeat of 'What's best for kids?' By the time [district officials] sent a letter home saying 'here's the program,' there was credibility that what's best for kids was actually [at the center of] the conversation."[12] Alonso stoked the community's latent hopes for their schools to gain support for his far-reaching initiatives. Having attended more than 120 PTA meetings during his first year as superintendent, he stated that "superintendents signal what they value by how they spend their time . . . I wanted to connect, I wanted the conversation to be iterative everywhere."

Alonso and his staff used the feedback from the meetings to inform their theory of change and strategy for the district: improve the school by substantially increasing the schools' authority to make decisions about budgeting, staffing, and the academic program. By establishing influential School Family Councils at each site, the district included families and communities in decisions about funding, curriculum, and the selection of principals. This strategy of increasing autonomy for the schools sent the message throughout the local community that family and community engagement would be at the center of the school improvement process, thus gradually changing expectations about what was possible among those constituents who could monitor their school's progress.

With these and other changes, high school dropout rates declined by 55 percent; graduation rates increased by more than 10 percent; students' tested performance improved in nearly all subjects and grades; and the district settled a twenty-eight-year-old federal lawsuit over special education services.[13] People working in the schools and in the central office reportedly no longer hid the fact that they worked for Baltimore City Schools; they felt proud to be a part of the improving system. The same central administrator quoted earlier said, "When we go to state meetings now, people are asking us, 'Well, how did you do x, y, and z?' because they're interested in knowing . . . We have broken through that layer of belief in ourselves and other people believing in us. People are confident in [Alonso's] ability, and they're confident that the organization is moving in the right direction, which allows us to make the natural mistakes that any other school system makes and not be vilified for them."

Baltimore's response to the conditions created by the external environment demonstrates how a district's theory of change and strategy can influence and gradually reset the environmental forces that affect it. Instead of ignoring or denying Baltimore's far-reaching reputation, the district's theory of change and corresponding strategies confronted it directly, changing practices both at the central office and in the schools. Working together, central administrators, principals, and teachers began to shift the beliefs, perceptions, and assumptions about the district. Baltimore was becoming a school district where people believed good things could happen.

Race and Social Class Affect Schooling in Charlotte-Mecklenburg and Montgomery County

In their recent report "Fifty Years after Brown: A Two-Tiered Education System," authors Carroll, Fulton, Abercrombie, and Yoon write that "fifty years after *Brown v. Board of Education*, unequal teaching and learning opportunities are still common in American schools. If we are serious about leaving no child behind, we must keep the promise of *Brown v. Board of Education* by ensuring that every school meets high standards."[14]

Leaders of each of the large, urban school districts we studied devised and developed a strategy for improvement that sat within the context of this nation's long and challenging history of race relations and social class dynamics in public schooling. Some were still responding to desegregation orders and busing plans that had been in place, either voluntarily or through court order, after states and communities sought to desegregate schools and offer equal educational opportunities to all students.

Districts also contended with the dynamics of disagreements and demands brought on by significant local shifts in racial, ethnic, and socioeconomic demographics. For example, neighborhoods in Long Beach varied markedly by income, and that inequality was reflected in the demographic profiles of their schools, creating the possibility that students would be far better served in some schools than others.

In response, the district's well-established approach of periodically reassigning all principals from school to school provided one means of equalizing the quality of leadership across the district. Through these regular shifts in administrative appointments, principals could see the range of schools and lived experiences, allowing them to understand and join the district's commitment to all students, wherever they were enrolled.

Drawing on examples from Charlotte-Mecklenburg and Montgomery County, we continue to explore how the environment—in this case, the intersection of race and class dynamics—can enable or disrupt a district's strategy for improvement. These cases illustrate how our nation's continuing struggle with issues of race and social class exerts a strong pull on the direction of decision making, strategy formation, and resource distribution in large, urban school districts. Given housing segregation and the prevalence of neighborhood schools, how school officials address these issues has far-reaching consequences for the central office–schools relationship.

Charlotte-Mecklenburg—Shifting Beliefs and Values about Desegregation. Charlotte-Mecklenburg has a long and complicated history with school desegregation and racial inequality. Like many public school districts in the South, it had failed to desegregate its schools even ten years after the Brown decision. The future of desegregation remained uncertain until the 1972 Supreme Court ruling on *Swann v. Charlotte-Mecklenburg Board of Education,* which found busing to be an appropriate solution to racial imbalance in the public schools. As a result, busing became widely used to integrate schools in the South, and Charlotte-Mecklenburg was viewed as a leader in ending segregated schools, earning it the reputation as "the city that made desegregation work."[15]

However, with Charlotte's rapid economic growth through the late 1980s into the 1990s, and with the arrival of many residents from the Northeast and Midwest, support for busing began to wane. In a 1992 effort to reduce the number of students being bused while also ensuring racial integration, Charlotte-Mecklenburg created a choice plan that included magnet schools and programs with quotas for white and black students. Some white families opposed the quota system, and in 1997, one parent sued the school system, claiming that his white daughter had been denied a seat in a magnet school because of her race. The case went to federal court and a judge ruled that Charlotte-Mecklenburg had met the mandates for desegregation and should stop using race as a factor in student assignment plans.

In 2002, Charlotte-Mecklenburg implemented a new student assignment plan, the Family Choice Plan, which split the district into four attendance zones based on neighborhoods; students could choose to stay in their neighborhood school or submit three ranked choices of other schools in the district.

When Gorman became superintendent in 2006, suburban parents, most of whom were white, were upset about the student assignment system and overcrowding in schools. At the same time, the business community criticized the poor performance of the district's high schools. Just before Gorman arrived, a bond referendum was rejected by more than 60 percent of voters—a strong sign that the community did not have confidence in the school system.

Although Gorman embarked on a fairly successful two-year public relations campaign to improve the image of the district, the issue of race continued to claim public attention. By 2010, the student assignment plan of 2002 no longer served to integrate the district, and the city's racial divides reemerged stronger than before. Gorman remarked, "Well, forty-five years later the county schools are saying, 'Hey, can't we jettison the city schools?' We've changed from this rural poverty and the inability for the county areas to carry their own in the early sixties to now where we're developing urban poverty and we have suburban sprawl. [Those in the suburbs are asking,] 'Can't we separate from that urban core?'"

In response to budget cuts, the district was forced to close schools; many of those they chose were in the city, serving majority poor and minority students. This exacerbated racial tensions and generated protests from local and state leaders of the NAACP, who filed a civil rights complaint with the U.S. Department of Education.

The case of Charlotte-Mecklenburg suggests several ways in which changes in the dynamics of race and class directly affected the relationship between the central office and the schools. The court ruling in 1997 led to the district dismantling the magnet school and quota system that it had relied on to desegregate schools. In response, the district moved to the Family Choice Plan, which emphasized neighborhood preference for schools. But because most of the low-income and minority students resided in the city center, while the white and wealthy students lived in the suburbs, "neighborhood choice" became a euphemism for segregating schools. To ensure equity across the segregated schools, the two superintendents before Gorman relied on centralized and standardized central office–schools relationships. For example, they implemented common curricula and pacing guides limiting the choices principals had over their academic programming. When this approach failed, the school board looked for a leader to implement a theory of change that emphasized decentralization. Thus, external social and legal forces have dramatically shaped the interactions between Charlotte-Mecklenburg's central office and its schools for over thirty years, a history that any superintendent would do well to know before taking action.

Montgomery County—Shifting Demographics and the Race/Class Narrative. Montgomery County also has long contended with issues of race and class, a struggle that has played out in its schools and their relationship with the central office. In the years before desegregation, Montgomery County had two separate school systems, one for black students and the other for white students. Schools for African Americans received proportionately less funding and had to put up with inferior facilities and instructional materials as well as lower pay for teachers.[16]

Soon after the *Brown v. Board of Education* decision in 1954, the school board voted to appoint a committee of African American and white school administrators to develop a plan for integration. By 1961, a slight majority of the district's schools were desegregated under the plan that relied on student transfers and busing to achieve more diverse student assignments. External community stakeholders exerted pressure on the district from both sides of the issue: the Montgomery County chapter of the NAACP repeatedly admonished the school board and administration for deliberately moving slowly to reduce inequities between whites and blacks, while local white dissenters protested the haste of the district's moves to integrate.[17]

By the 1980s, the minority populations of African Americans, Hispanics, and Asians had doubled. Despite this, the district experienced continued resistance to its desegregation efforts from newly elected board members who had campaigned to eliminate "forced busing" and "social engineering."[18] The board members successfully eliminated some busing plans, disbanded the board's minority relations committee, and abolished a mandatory course on black culture for Montgomery County teachers.[19] And like Charlotte-Mecklenburg, Montgomery County was forced to abandon its practice of using race as a determining factor for school admission after a white parent filed a federal lawsuit in 1997 when his child was not allowed to transfer to another school because the transfer would violate a 1980 policy to prevent racial segregation.[20]

Two decades later, the district was still responding to the issues of race and social class in its community. By 1999, Montgomery County's white student population had shrunk from 62 percent in 1990 to 52 percent, while the overall student population had grown by 21 percent.[21] Recognizing the steady increase in minority students, newly appointed superintendent Jerry Weast sought to build a sense of urgency in the community to support district reforms that would reduce the achievement gap between majority and minority students.

In order to highlight attention to the high correlation between low performing schools and concentrations of minority populations, administrators created a map that geographically divided the district into two zones, Red and Green, based on socioeconomic indicators. The maps served as a starting point for helping stakeholders understand how the district might differentiate resources and management across schools. Using the maps and data to galvanize support from racially and socioeconomically diverse community stakeholders, union leaders, and board members, the administration produced and widely distributed "A Call to Action: Raising the Bar, Closing the Gap" in November 1999. District leaders began a new, frank dialogue about issues of race and class with a focus on reducing institutional barriers to improved achievement for all students, and they instituted the tight accountability and monitoring relationship between the district and the schools that would be in place for over a decade.[22]

Superintendent Josh Starr subsequently sought to reorient this accountability and monitoring system in a way that would better generate equity and innovation. However, a decision to ease up on accountability could not be made lightly, given that the practices originally were based in efforts to eliminate disadvantages that were grounded in racial and social class differences. When we visited, some administrators expressed fear that, without tight expectations of accountability between the central office and the schools, the inequities that they had fought hard to reduce would reemerge. It will take some time to determine whether Starr's shift away from the district's traditional approach to accountability would, in fact, undermine the equity that had been achieved in the schools over the past decade.

SUMMARY

As much as district leaders may employ various strategies to support the schools, strong external forces—economic, legal, political, social, and cultural—can disrupt their pursuit of improvement through coherence. If central office leaders fail to acknowledge or understand these features of the external environment, they may champion unworkable strategies that are impossible to fund or difficult for principals and teachers to implement, or they will be unlikely to receive support from the community or public officials. Ill-suited plans and programs are likely to erode, rather than enhance, the much-needed trust between the central office and the schools. However, a thoughtful understanding of the external environment increases the likelihood that district leaders will make the most of what they have to support teaching and learning in the schools.

It's important that district and school leaders realize that the external environment is dynamic—things can change, and they often do. Those responsible for the district must continuously monitor the complex, nuanced, and ever-changing forces in the environment, paying special attention to less commonly recognized factors, such as the history of race and class in the community and its schools. Any plan, however well-grounded and carefully developed, can be upended by the unanticipated effects of an election upset, a sudden downturn in the economy, the repeal of a law, a social crisis, or the unexpected arrival of a new group of immigrants. In fact, several such changes may occur at the same time. Therefore, district leaders must be attentive, agile, and ready to work together to adjust their local policies and practices so that they will better meet the needs of all students in all schools.

LESSONS FOR PRACTICE

Before making decisions about structure and strategy, leaders need to have a deep understanding of the environment in which their district operates. Because many superintendents have never worked in the district they head, this requires deliberately learning about conditions, past and present, that local employees and citizens often take for granted. If the district's strategy for managing schools and improving schooling is to work, it must be (or become) coherent with the environment as well as with other organizational elements, such as structures, resources, and systems. With that in mind, we suggest the following:

- *Take time to study the environment of your district.* Draw on as many sources as you can—books, media accounts, interviews, focus groups, surveys—to learn about the external factors that might advance or stifle your efforts. Although school boards and local communities are often impatient for answers, blueprints, and results, it's a mistake to assume that you can skip such thorough, open inquiry.

- *In developing a strategy for central office–schools relationships, consider whether parts of your plans are vulnerable to threats from changes in the environment.* For example, what assumptions do you have about continued funding or ongoing support by board members? Conversely, anticipate whether some actions or initiatives might get a boost from a newly elected official, incentives included in a state law, or community groups that promote similar goals. As with organizational culture, the environment can be a constraining or enabling force on a district's theory of change and strategy.

⊃ *Develop the capacity in district and school leaders to examine environmental forces.* Creating a strategy that is nimble and responsive to the environment requires leaders who pay attention and can anticipate how external forces influence the relationship between the central office and the schools. School districts must ensure that district and school leaders are competent not only in examining the external environment but also in seeing opportunities to integrate insights about those external factors into the district's strategy.

⊃ *Set up structures and systems that continuously gather information about the external environment.* Districts can use formal partnerships with schools, local unions, families, and community members to learn about the external forces shaping work. Similarly, district leaders manage up by connecting with state and federal policy makers to influence policies and statutes that might affect the district.

Conclusion

In 1848, Horace Mann extolled public education as "the great equalizer of the conditions of men." More than 160 years later, economic inequality persists and widens, reminding us that far too many students—especially those who attend high-poverty, urban schools—don't get the education they deserve. Righting that injustice now, sixty years after state-sponsored segregation in our public schools was ruled unconstitutional, requires improving instruction for every student in every classroom of every school. Given how large, complex, and varied urban districts are, this is an enormously difficult task. It was this goal of achieving excellence at scale and the challenges districts face in doing so that motivated this research.

In our study of five large, urban school districts—all recognized for their performance and improvement—we focused on the relationship between the central office and the schools. Although authority for managing the school district rests in the central office, the essential work of teaching and learning happens within the schools. We wanted to understand and explain how central officials managed important decisions and day-to-day work with scores of principals, thousands of teachers, tens of thousands of students, and a wide range of local communities. Was there a one-best-strategy that others could use successfully to manage similarly complex and challenging school districts?

We learned that there was no single strategy that would allow all districts to realize the equalizing power of public education that

Horace Mann foresaw. Nor was there a single theory of change that could reliably guide education leaders' efforts across all districts. Three of the districts we studied had achieved notable growth and success by grounding their strategies in the promise of centralization—where the decision rights for the important matters of budgeting, staffing, and academic programming were largely held by administrators in the central office. Two other districts, also recognized for their accomplishments and progress, believed in decentralization—which called for delegating to principals decisions about this same set of strategic priorities. All districts had experienced both successes and setbacks with their favored approaches.

We also learned that not any strategy will do. Assembling a set of promising actions and activities without thoughtful coordination leads to organizational incoherence, making it hard to get things done throughout the district. Without coherence, policies intended to spur creative action instead reward principals for gaming the system and often generate troubling inequities across schools. Those meant to bring order unintentionally lead to stagnation and schools' lack of responsiveness to the unique needs of their students and communities. In such cases, the basic elements of the organization (structures, systems, and resources) work in isolation or at cross-purposes. Meanwhile, the strategic priorities—those policies and practices of budgeting, staffing, and academic programming that most directly affect students' experiences—are incompatible. As a result, the efforts of everyone—from central administrators, to principals, to teachers— are squandered, and the school district achieves far less for its students than it might. Therefore, in selecting a theory of change and strategy, district leaders must be attentive, responsive, and deliberate in designing and supporting a coherent system for managing central office–schools relationships.

CENTRALIZATION OR DECENTRALIZATION?

Overall, the practical, working relationships that these districts developed inclined toward either centralization or decentralization, though every district's policies and practices included some mix of both approaches. The accounts of those we interviewed, history of educational change, and recent research about school district organization suggest that it is unwise for district administrators to totally control school-based practices (rigorous centralization) or to grant unbridled autonomy to every school (radical decentralization).

Reliance on rigorous centralization incorrectly assumes that schools and the communities they serve are so alike that they would be well served by a standardized strategy. Moreover, it assumes that central office leaders could, if they chose, control practices throughout all schools. We know from research on program implementation that this is an unrealistic expectation, especially in large and complex systems. A rigorously centralized—and therefore top-down—system fails to benefit from the expertise and ingenuity of its principals and teachers, who have valuable insights and recommendations for improving a district's approach. District officials' efforts to control education from the central office too often generate disappointment, cynicism, and disengagement among those who work most closely with students.

At the same time, relying on radical decentralization by devolving all authority to autonomous schools can create serious problems of inefficiency and inequity across the school district. Every school has to acquire skilled personnel to budget and allocate resources; recruit, screen, hire, and evaluate teachers; select and implement curriculum; and assess students' progress. Few urban schools have sufficient administrative support and expertise to carry out these functions, and it is costly and inefficient for a district to dedicate staff time and training to acquire them. In radically decentralized districts, individual schools are responsible only to their local community, not to the greater good of the district. This arrangement leads schools to be self-serving in their choices and runs the risk of replicating the have and have-not patterns of inequity that persist in large, urban districts today. Without attention and support, low-income communities lack the political influence of schools in wealthier communities. They are unlikely to secure first-rate facilities, enterprising principals, and accomplished teachers.

Today, there is growing interest in granting more schools in urban districts greater autonomy. In this study, we found promising efforts under way to decentralize the school systems in Charlotte-Mecklenburg and Baltimore and learned about many reported benefits for students in the purposefully centralized Aldine, Long Beach, and Montgomery County districts. We found that when these approaches worked well, the districts had incorporated ways to guard against the problems associated with either rigorous centralization or radical decentralization.

In order for strategies grounded in decentralization to work, districts had to consider how to maintain principals' concern for the greater good of the district. They also had to prepare principals to effectively use their autonomy, which meant providing training, advice, and active assistance by intermediaries from the central office. For example, district officials in Baltimore City created network teams of specialists to support principals as they created their budgets, hired staff, and made crucial decisions about their academic program. Such support was especially important to principals when their schools faced new challenges that required extensive expertise, such as implementing the Common Core State Standards. Expertise was necessary at all levels so that schools could successfully exercise their new decision rights.

At the same time, introducing school-site autonomy that was bounded by "guidance" from Baltimore's central office gave some assurance to district officials that principals would make choices that were in line with best practices, the interests of their students, and the concerns of their communities. In Charlotte-Mecklenburg, however, district officials did not support the Strategic Staffing Initiative with systems that ensured all participating principals could recruit and select high-quality teaching teams to accompany them to their assigned struggling school. And without that support system in place, the program failed to achieve its potential.

When centralized approaches worked, central office officials sought to understand the needs, views, and practice-based wisdom of those in the schools as they developed standards and programs to be implemented throughout the district. Long Beach, for example, routinely pilot-tested and refined programs before expecting all schools to adopt them. In Montgomery County, teachers and principals held influential roles on committees and task forces that defined the poli-cies and practices that were then used districtwide. These school dis-tricts took deliberate steps to become well-informed by those who were most deeply involved in, and knowledgeable about, students' learning. However, Aldine's single-minded focus on the state tests in Texas reportedly led district officials there to ignore or limit feed-back from teachers about central office mandates for curriculum and pedagogy. Thus, when centralization worked, it was not exercised as rigid, top-down control but as an effort to inform the district's poli-cies and practices by soliciting and responding to advice from those in the schools.

ACHIEVING COHERENCE

Given that neither rigorous centralization nor radical decentraliza-tion works, what should district leaders do? What should they try to achieve? How can they know what works in managing their cen-tral office–schools relationships? Our research and experience with many large, urban districts suggest that district leaders should strive to achieve *coherence.*

It's important to understand that the parts of a coherent system are coordinated and compatible but not necessarily aligned tightly. Even in the most closely monitored and uniformly managed edu-cational systems, schools remain distinctive. Because schools must function effectively in their own local context, they have important features that remain only loosely coupled to the larger organization.[1] Although some reformers might try to achieve full alignment across all programs, practices, and schools, tight coupling across the district discourages accommodation in response to the inevitable variation among so many unique schools. In fact, routine and complete com-pliance with central office mandates can impede coherence by pre-cluding "mutual adaptation," the process by which both policies and institutions change during effective implementation.[2]

In practice, what it means to achieve coherence in the central office–schools relationship differs across districts, for it is contin-gent on a district's theory of change, bound up in its strategy, and dependent on a host of environmental factors. Coherence or lack of coherence is apparent in the relationships among the parts and processes that the district adopts to enact its strategy. When the pieces are sensibly arranged and mutually reinforcing, the system makes progress toward its goal of improving instruction and learning for every child in every school. When they are not, progress is stalled or declines.

We found that districts had to achieve coherence among the organizational elements used to change how things are done. These include a district's systems, structures, and resources. For example, Aldine committed central office resources to a national teacher recruitment system that attracted strong candidates from first-rate teacher preparation programs. Principals then were given responsibility to choose the teachers who had the skills and attitudes needed to improve their students' performance on state tests. Baltimore moved responsibility for managing resources to the schools, created a network system to assist principals in budgeting, and required that budgets not be submitted without the endorsement of parents. With these related activities, Baltimore effectively implemented its strategy of bounded autonomy. In very different ways, both districts achieved coherence, not only among the organizational elements of systems, structures, and resources but also among the strategic priorities of budgeting, staffing, and academic programming.

In assessing coherence, it is important to judge what actually happens and not rely solely on written testimony. Formal documents that principals and their staff prepare in order to demonstrate that their requests or activities align with the district's goals or strategic plan may be misleading or incomplete. Principals in Charlotte-Mecklenburg told of spending considerable time justifying their requests to spend Title I funds, yet they did not suggest that this task accomplished anything beyond securing the funds. Requiring principals to document how their decisions align with the district's strategic plan may be just an exercise in compelling compliance, not a move toward achieving coherence.

Coherence may be hard to see, but it is not invisible to those who spend their time in schools. For this reason, the role of intermediaries can be very informative and constructive. These agents of the central office who are active and present in the schools can discover unforeseen synergies and identify mismatched strategies and, in the process, can see what works and what doesn't. The information they glean as they seek to understand why some efforts fail and others succeed is valuable to both central office and school leaders as they seek to achieve coherence.

Coherence between the central office and the schools can improve not only how resources are used, decisions are made, and services are provided (making them more effective, efficient, and equitable), but it also can enhance the district's capacity to respond to new policies, opportunities, or threats. When we visited Aldine, Texas was in the process of implementing a new, more rigorous test, the State of Texas Assessments of Academic Readiness. Central office administrators and principals expressed confidence that the district would be able to meet the demands of the test after a period of adjustment. As one central office administrator remarked, "We're going to regroup. We're already in the process of regrouping. Of course, you know the cutoff is going to be very low in the beginning, but we will make adjustments. We will redesign our district improvement plan. We'll roll it out to the campus like we did with TAKS and we will make the adjustment." As Aldine illustrates, coherence is a process rather than an end state. Districts that are intent on improving and refining the relationship between the central office and the schools will always be *approaching* coherence, not declaring coherence. They will continue efforts to make their systems, structures, and resources more compatible and their approaches to budgeting, staffing, and academic programming mutually supportive and reinforcing.

Some tension will always exist between the priorities and expectations of district officials and those of principals. Even in districts with highly coherent organizations, these administrators have shared, though not identical, interests. The principal's primary allegiance will be to her school rather than to the district. For this reason, we view the principals as stakeholders in the system, advocating and acting on behalf of their teachers, students, and parents, even as they work to implement the district's plans within their schools. In the ongoing relationship between the central office and the schools, this tension may actually provide evidence of coherence rather than incoherence. When central office and school leaders see a problem or opportunity differently, it may be that both are right and that a more complex understanding of what's happening and what's possible will lead to decisions that serve students better.

In Long Beach, for example, central office officials piloted a new program that placed all students in danger of failing eighth grade (i.e., those with two or more Fs) into one school. The belief was that they could then concentrate resources in this one school to support struggling students. However, the principal and teachers at the school helped the central office understand why the plan was flawed. The students were in danger of failing out for a wide variety of reasons—health issues, instability at home, drug and alcohol addictions, and undiagnosed learning disabilities, to name a few. Central office administrators listened to these concerns and ended the program. As Long Beach superintendent Chris Steinhauser remarked, "The school actually came to us and said, 'This is a disaster. We need to rethink this whole process.' We've made some blunders, to be honest with you, but we also try, whatever we do, to try to build on what we already have."

The tension between the central office and the schools will continue as long as there are systems of schools that are centrally governed. It can be a creative tension that informs the larger system, one that is generative and constructive. Yet, to be productive, those who work throughout the system must trust the good intentions of others and have confidence that they will keep their word and do as they promise.

LEVERS OF CHANGE

We have identified the important elements of the central office–schools relationship based on the advice of district teams participating in our PELP summer institute as well as on our own knowledge and experience. We sought to focus on the decisions that both the central office and the schools had a stake in—those in staffing, budgeting, and academic programming—because they had the greatest effect on students' learning. Our interviews with central office and school-site administrators confirmed that these strategic priorities were, indeed, of great concern and consequence since they determined how successful the district and the schools would be in improving performance and achieving equity. These decisions were also interdependent: resources were allocated to support hiring staff and purchasing instructional materials; teachers were chosen because they showed promise as inspiring, effective instructors; and the academic program provided curriculum to guide those teachers' pedagogy and assess their students' progress. Where and how well decisions were made by central office and school leaders about these three aspects of the district's strategy determined a great deal about students' opportunities and success as learners. Therefore, we assert that the three strategic priorities are the most obvious and important levers for improvement available to the central office and school leaders who share responsibility for managing them.

We provided in the earlier chapters many instructive examples of how the strategic priorities interacted, either productively or unproductively, in the districts we studied. Aldine, Long Beach, and Montgomery County recruited and hired teachers who had experiences and skills that reinforced features of the academic program. Baltimore gave principals control over their budgets so they could hire staff into special community-liaison roles. Charlotte released principals from standardized curricula to spur innovative teaching. These suggest how thoughtful school administrators can ensure that students benefit from well-managed decisions, whether the district chooses a theory of change that is inclined toward centralization or decentralization.

Our research also highlights the potential of organizational culture as a lever for change. As we have suggested, culture is often unappreciated and underused. However, it is not optional. Every district has a culture that creates opportunities and constraints for anyone intent on instituting change. A district's culture may be a strong one with shared values and high commitment, or it may be a weak one that is diffuse or contested. Norms and values can minimize the need for close oversight of school practices and serve reformers well when the culture is strong and positive. However, strong cultures also can be problematic when the deeply held beliefs of principals, teachers, or school communities run counter to practices that district leaders hope to promote. Most importantly, violating established cultural norms can derail any superintendent's carefully designed and well-intentioned plans. Therefore, understanding a district's organizational culture is well worth the investment, especially if new district administrators are recruited from outside the district and, therefore, do not know it well.

It's worth remembering that culture itself is subject to change. Declaring a culture change won't work, but taking actions that signal a new culture can. If a district's culture is marked by distrust—as Baltimore's was when Andrés Alonso arrived—the simple (though time-consuming) act of meeting and listening carefully to constituents can generate trust that supports subsequent initiatives. Changes in systems, structures, or resources also can lead to shifts in values and norms in the district's culture. A district where central office administrators routinely play principals off against each other is likely to have a culture of unhealthy competition, one in which principals lack any sense of responsibility for the general good of the district. However, a new superintendent can institute a fair and transparent system for distributing resources, which not only changes who gets what but also conveys clearly that those who act responsibly will be treated well. Thus, practice can change culture.

The external environment, however, is less amenable to change by district leaders. For the most part, superintendents have little or no influence over sudden changes in the economy, established social or cultural practices in the community, or new federal policies that specify how students will be assessed and school districts judged. Still, superintendents of large, urban districts can have important influence on state legislatures and local politics by regularly asserting the stake that the government has in having an effective education system. In responding to the changes in the environment, they can take a variety of actions that reduce or augment the effects of the change.

STABILITY AND CHANGE OVER TIME

From the beginning of this study, we knew that we wanted to visit school districts that enjoyed reasonable stability over time. Districts that experience frequent turnover in the superintendent's office also often lose others from their cabinet who head key departments. We didn't set out to consider the importance of stability, but we did learn how important it is in building culture, promoting trust, instituting change, and sustaining improvements.

Three districts—Aldine, Long Beach, and Montgomery County—experienced a decade or more of continuity at the central office and on the school board. Over time, stability and success seemed to be mutually reinforcing. Success was apparent in these districts' improved structures and systems; more targeted, purposeful use of resources; and notable improvement in student performance. Surely those accomplishments made it possible for leaders in these districts to keep their jobs and find them rewarding. When Wanda Bamberg and Chris Steinhauser were promoted from within to become super-intendents, their appointments signaled an endorsement of the district's current approaches to managing the schools. When Jerry Weast retired from Montgomery County, the district hired Josh Starr with the expectation that he would move the district ahead on much the same course.

In only one of the districts, Charlotte-Mecklenburg, did the school board or local politicians suddenly shift the educational priorities and expectations. Critics might well suggest that such continuity of leadership and programs stifles reform. However, developing a coherent and productive relationship between the central office and the schools takes time. A fully coherent set of structures, systems, and resources does not appear ready-made for installation. Instead, it is developed over time through thoughtful planning, trial and error, regular review, and ongoing refinement. Coherence emerges not as whim or chance but as a consequence of steady, deliberate efforts.

The contrast between the stability of those districts and instability of Baltimore when Alonso became superintendent is noteworthy.

Rather than being hired to sustain success, he was expected to create order and generate improvement in a failing system that had run through seven superintendents in ten years. The challenge was daunting, but Alonso saw that the community was ready for serious change, and he had backing from his school board. After listening carefully to the concerns of stakeholders and many in the community, he acted decisively to reduce the size of the central office, replace ineffective principals, hire new central administrators, change the formula for funding schools, and grant bounded autonomy to schools. The pace of change was said by those involved to be both breathtaking and exhilarating. The results, as measured in student test scores, reduced suspensions, and graduation rates, were impressive.

Alonso's experience suggests that it is possible to substantially, positively change the working relationship between the central office and the schools in several years of very intense work. However, after seven years Alonso resigned, and soon after many of his central administrators left. It is not yet clear what that change in administration will mean for Baltimore and whether the reforms Alonso introduced will be sustained and further developed or renounced and abandoned. The carefully cultivated values of shared responsibility, initiative, high expectations, and respect for parents that Alonso nourished in Baltimore will not easily be supplanted. But the school-based decision rights of principals to build their budgets, hire their teachers, and select their curricula can be rescinded. In time, it will become clear whether these fundamental changes in Baltimore's central office–schools relationship will stand.

The case of Charlotte-Mecklenburg raises different concerns about stability. Peter Gorman was superintendent for five years before he resigned unexpectedly in 2011. While his predecessors had sought to centralize and standardize practice across the county's many schools, Gorman was hired with a mandate to change course, which he did with various initiatives meant to grant more discretion to schools, especially in staffing and academic programming. He encountered some resistance from principals who were accustomed to a district culture that ostensibly called for compliance but tolerated rebellion. His reforms—Freedom and Flexibility and the

Strategic Staffing Initiative—were unevenly implemented and not well established when he left the district. It is not clear whether Charlotte-Mecklenburg Schools will again reverse direction and centralize practice or continue shifting more responsibility and autonomy to successful schools. Had Gorman's reforms achieved sufficient success and endorsement to sustain them over time? A somewhat tumultuous five-year tenure may have been insufficient to fundamentally redirect the district's theory of change and strategy. Much will depend on the priorities and decisions of Gorman's successor.

Achieving stability over time can help create clear expectations and a predictable work environment for administrators and teachers, while unexpected, rapid change can inure people to the excitement and promise of having new options. Faced with yet another reform, those in the schools are inclined to put their heads down and close their doors rather than embrace an unexpected opportunity. Continuity of leadership and strategy prepare people to respond purposefully, rather than react unpredictably, to the demands of a dynamic environment. It also helps build a strong, positive culture that can sustain a district through difficult times by promoting respect, trust, and shared responsibility.

It's important to add that this call for stability is not an endorsement of stagnancy. "Staying the course" does not mean holding tightly and fervently to whatever is in place. In some cases it's necessary to disrupt a system, as Alonso did in downsizing his central office and pushing responsibility to principals who were accustomed to being told what to do. In other cases, disrupting the system might lead to confusion, which then has to be managed carefully with clear communication about values, priorities, and acceptable practice.

THE MISSION OF LARGE, URBAN SCHOOL DISTRICTS

The findings of our study are relevant for any school district—large, medium, or small, urban, suburban, or rural. We are convinced that everyone benefits from working in a system that establishes a coherent, dynamic, and responsive relationship between central administrators and those in the schools. However, establishing such a relationship is especially critical for large, urban districts. These school systems serve large numbers of low-income students of color, whose needs have long been neglected or their interests overrun by the priorities and politics of those in higher-income neighborhoods. Given that housing in large, urban districts typically is segregated by race, ethnicity, and social class, local schools usually differ markedly from one another in the students they serve. Left to themselves, the district's schools are likely to eventually mirror many of the strengths and weaknesses of the communities they serve: parents in higher-income, white neighborhoods garner a large share of resources, services, and attention while parents in lower-income, minority neighborhoods do not get what their children deserve. Although districts with fair-minded leaders may seek to diversify student assignments to schools, the practical and legal challenges of desegregation and the sobering reality of resegregation remind us how important it is to manage resources and opportunities so that they increase equity across all schools, whatever their composition. Doing so will continue to be a primary responsibility for central office and school leaders of large, urban districts in the foreseeable future. The challenge of achieving equity, therefore, rests in how a district manages its many schools and serves its various communities.

Methodology

Our study emerged from discussing problems of practice with district leaders who attended our annual PELP summer institute. Many raised questions about how to manage the relationship between the central office and the schools: Where should decisions be made? Where does the greater capacity to improve performance exist, in the central office or the principal's office? At which level of the system should more authority rest, the top or the bottom? Will centralized or decentralized decision-making lead to higher performance across schools?

In the fall of 2010, the PELP team launched this study in order to better understand what lay behind these questions and how we might respond to them. We first talked with leaders in the field and then reviewed the literature on school effectiveness and district-level strategy. Based on that preliminary work, we prepared two annotated bibliographies and a tentative framework that included the key dimensions of policy and practice that are of shared interest to central office and school-side administrators. This eventually served as the basis for identifying our three strategic priorities—budgeting, staffing, and academic programming.

SITE SELECTION

We then engaged in an iterative process of site selection. We wanted to have a small sample of large, urban districts that had demonstrated success and/or accelerated progress in improving outcomes for students. We were not, however, intending to explain the successes of exemplary districts; rather, we wanted to explore the experiences of central office administrators and principals in managing their central office–schools relationships. It made sense to focus on districts that generally were regarded as effective. We began with a list of sixty potential sites and gradually narrowed that down to fourteen districts that met our general criteria. We then collected as much information as we could about these districts' demographics, finances, leadership, governance, and student achievement. Because we wanted to study districts that approached the issue of central office–schools relationships intentionally, we also looked closely at the districts' published strategies and underlying theories of change.

In March 2011 we identified five large, urban districts as a tentative sample. They varied in location, relevant state laws, growth or decline in size, demographic makeup of students, and tenure of the superintendent, but all had experienced stability or continuity of leadership over the past five to ten years. Three districts reported relying on a centralized approach to managing their central office–schools relationships, while the other two had recently moved toward decentralization. All five superintendents agreed to participate.

The study design reflected a case study approach. We integrated news sources, research reports, and Web-based material with in-person interviews with principals, area superintendents, and senior leaders. Beginning in the spring of 2011 and continuing for a year, a PELP research team that included members from both the Harvard education and business schools visited the districts and conducted interviews for two to four days. In each district we first interviewed the superintendent, deputy superintendents, and several area superintendents in their offices. We then traveled to the schools to interview the principals at their sites. In all, we interviewed sixty-three district and school leaders (thirty-two central office administrators and thirty-one principals). We also collected more than 2,200 pages of district documents, research reports, news articles, and case studies on these five districts.

PARTICIPANTS

Within each district we sought to interview a diverse group of administrators who had different experiences and could offer varying perspectives on how the district leaders managed the central office–schools relationship. In recruiting participants, we contacted a district liaison in the central office and asked to interview the superintendent, deputy superintendent, assistant superintendent of curriculum and instruction, two to four regional superintendents, and six to eight principals.

Our district liaison decided which area superintendents to include in our sample. In developing the sample of principals, we asked to speak with a variety of individuals who headed schools that were located in different neighborhoods, served different grade levels (elementary, middle, and high), and had demonstrated different levels of student achievement. We realized that we might be steered to speak only with principals who endorsed the work of central administrators and, therefore, repeatedly asked to speak with principals who held differing views. We reviewed the demographics and student test performance of the principals' schools in each district's sample and confirmed that they reflected a wide range of student composition and academic achievement. In order to be sure that principals did not feel coerced by our district liaison to participate, we explained to all individuals that participation was voluntary and that they could withdraw from the study at any point.

INTERVIEWS

We developed different interview protocols for superintendents, central office administrators, and principals (see table A.1). Generally, we asked the participants to describe and reflect on the working relationship between the central office and the schools. We inquired about the district's overall approach in managing that relationship and posed more specific questions about how decisions were made regarding the strategic priorities of budgeting, staffing, and the academic program.

TABLE A.1 Interview questions for principals, central office administrators, and superintendents

PRINCIPALS	CENTRAL OFFICE ADMINISTRATORS	SUPERINTENDENTS
Could you describe your district's strategy?	Could you describe your district's strategy?	Could you describe your district's strategy?
Your schools all have different performance levels, capacities, communities, and demographics. How do you think about adapting your district's strategy to these varying school needs? What are the advantages and disadvantages to this approach?	Your schools all have different performance levels, capacities, communities, and demographics. How do you think about adapting your district's strategy to these varying school needs? What are the advantages and disadvantages to this approach?	Your schools all have different performance levels, capacities, communities, and demographics. How do you think about adapting your district's strategy to these varying school needs? What are the advantages and disadvantages to this approach? What are the key challenges for implementing this strategy?
How would you describe your relationship with central office? What do you rely on central office for?	If you think about school autonomy on a continuum, with high school autonomy on one end and low school autonomy on the other, where would you put your district's schools? Are there certain areas where schools have more or less autonomy? Can you give me an example?	Of the many things going on in your school district, which ones do you feel have the greatest effect on student learning?
If you think about school autonomy on a continuum, with high school autonomy on one end and low school autonomy on the other, where would you put your school? Are there certain areas where your school has more or less autonomy?	What role does central office play in staffing, curriculum and instruction, budgeting?	If you think about school autonomy on a continuum, with high school autonomy on one end and low school autonomy on the other, where would you put your district's schools? Are there certain areas where schools have more or less autonomy?
How much control do you have over your school's budget? What can you control? What role does central office play in your school's budget? What aspects of the budget do you not have control over? Is it important to your job?	How would you describe your relationship with principals?	What role does central office play in staffing, curriculum and instruction, budgeting?

TABLE A.1   Interview questions for principals, central office
administrators, and superintendents, *continued*

PRINCIPALS	CENTRAL OFFICE ADMINISTRATORS	SUPERINTENDENTS
How much control do you have over staffing (typical year before the budget crisis): What role does central office play in staffing? What aspects of staffing do you not have control over? Is it important to your job?	How would you describe your relationship with central office?	What is consistent across schools? What is variable?
What decisions can you make about your school's curriculum and instruction? What role does central office play in curriculum and instruction? What curriculum and instruction decisions do you not have control over? Are these important to your job?	How do you manage that relationship between central office and schools? Could you give an example of when there was tension between central office and school principals? How did you manage that tension?	How do you recruit principals? What are you looking for in a principal?
How much control do you have over the school's schedule and how time is allocated? What role does central office play in the school schedule? What scheduling decisions do you not have control over? Are these important to your job?	Is there anything else we haven't asked that you think is important for us to know about your district?	Do you have systems in place to create a principal pipeline? What kind of training do they receive? How do you evaluate principals? What do you do about principals who need help?
How much control do you have over the management structures and the policies and practices of your school? What role does central office play in the school's governance? What governance decisions do you not have control over? Are these important to your job?	Do you have any questions you'd like to ask us?	Is there anything else we haven't asked that you think is important for us to know about your district?
What is important for us to know about the work of being a principal in [district name] today?		Do you have any questions you'd like to ask us?
Do you have any questions you'd like to ask us?		

We provided our participants with different assurances about anonymity and confidentiality based on their position. We informed superintendents that because of the public quasi-political nature of their position, their responses would not be anonymous. We explained that we would use their names in quoting them, but we promised not to quote, attribute, or discuss with others any comments they made about individuals in the district. Similarly, we explained to other central office administrators (associate superintendents, deputy superintendents, chiefs, and assistant superintendents) that we might quote them by name but that we would not discuss their comments with others we interviewed. We assured principals that we would not use their names or identifying characteristics in our writing and that we would not discuss their responses with anyone else in the district.

ANALYSIS

We digitally recorded, transcribed, and loaded all the interviews into the qualitative software analysis program Atlas TI. We analyzed the interview data in two phases. First, we identified broad themes from the interviews and then used those to write summaries about what we had learned about each district's structure and organization, organizational culture, and central office–school relationship, especially decisions about academic programming, budgeting, and staffing.

We then developed an initial set of codes based on the themes emerging from our summaries as well as codes based on prior research about site-based school management.[1] We reviewed and refined our approach to coding several times and eventually wrote analytical memos for each district, focusing on the key themes that emerged from the coded data. Our final set of codes is presented in table A.2. These analytic themes included theory of change, budgeting, staffing, curriculum and instruction, and culture. As we analyzed, wrote, and discussed what we had learned, we found the PELP Coherence Framework to be a useful tool for an organizing and understanding our findings.

TABLE A.2   Codes and descriptions

CODE	DESCRIPTION
Accountability	Specific explanations of holding others accountable or being held accountable; discussions of culture of accountability; references to expectations set by district leadership
Assessment	Descriptions of any type of assessment (benchmarking, formative, and summative) and how they are used in the district or school; also includes any discussions about the state assessment, including references to subgroup performance and Adequate Yearly Progress (AYP)
Budgeting	Includes the budgeting process, how funds are allocated to specific departments or programs, resources for supplies and materials, discussions of federal or state categorical funds, and mention of private donations; also includes discussions of budget cuts. Budget cuts may force superintendents or principals to make certain decisions. The cuts may be because of declining enrollments, economic downturn, or changes in state or federal funding formulas.
Curriculum and instruction	Discussions of curriculum content (tools, resources, material, and texts), pacing (rate at which the standards and content are taught), standards (what a student should know and be able to do by a certain grade or age), and programs (supplemental math, literacy, or science programs); also, content about instructional approach a teacher actually uses in the classroom
District–school relationship	Descriptions of relationships and communication between district and schools; rather than specific decisions this code includes general discussions of relationships and communication pathways between district and schools (for example, it includes general discussions of who communicates with whom and why, and discussions of whether "ask for permission or forgiveness")
Environment	Anything pertaining to the surrounding context of school districts and schools. Including formal and informal state and local politics and state statutes; public and media perception of the school district; the degree to which the public supports the school district; also includes demographic information about the school district and schools; discussions about charter schools are also captured with this code
Equity	Concerns issues of resource distribution between low-income and high-income communities in the district and people's perceptions of the policies; specifically, discussions of inequality in resources including money, supplies, supplemental programs, teaching positions across different schools in district
Leadership	Discussions of desired and actual style, traits, hiring, training, and succession planning of assistant principals, principals, and central office administrators; broad descriptions of how principals think about their job and what they actually do; includes references to the implicit or explicit processes or strategy for how leadership positions are filled in the district

(continued)

TABLE A.2 Codes and descriptions, *continued*

CODE	DESCRIPTION
Scheduling	Process and references to school schedules including start and end times, minutes allotted for particular subjects, and degree of flexibility in setting the schedule; can be used as a double code with curriculum instruction or staffing support to denote amount of time spent on certain subjects or time used for professional development, respectively
School board	References to school board composition, stability, and policies
Staffing evaluation	Specific references to the process or instrument used for teacher evaluation; includes discussions of changes in teacher evaluation and how teachers react to evaluation; also, any descriptions of teacher dismissal procedures
Staffing hiring and assignment	Descriptions of how teaching positions are allotted and filled including recruitment, screening, hiring, and placement processes; also specific discussions of difficulty filling positions; includes descriptions of experiences, knowledge, skills, and dispositions desired in teacher hires
Staffing support	Informal and formal training to update the knowledge and skills of experienced and new teachers; includes support provided by central office staff, outside consultants, professional learning communities, peers/mentors, coaches, and school-level leaders
Strategy	Descriptions of the district's espoused strategies or theories of change; also, includes discussions of changes in strategy and comparisons with other districts' strategies
Student assignment	The process in which a district assigns students to schools and the consequences associated with the assignment process

Finally, our collaborative writing process reflected the core strength of PELP. The five coauthors, who come from education and business, approached the project with diverse backgrounds, priorities, and tastes. Different, sometimes competing, views emerged. We harnessed this tension with open and critical discussions in meetings and through close review of our chapter drafts.

NOTES

INTRODUCTION

1. Arika Herron, "Emory Outlines Goals before School Board," *Winston-Salem Journal,* September 25, 2013.
2. "Head of Ky.'s Public Schools Warns State Will Take Over Struggling Schools If It Must," February 13, 2013, *Associated Press.*
3. Jefferson County School District, "Strategic Plan: Vision 2015," http://issuu .com/jcps-ky/docs/vision2015_8.3.12_1_?e=3222915/2022051.
4. Caitlin Farrell et al., *Scaling Up Charter Management Organizations: Eight Key Lessons for Success* (Los Angeles: National Resource Center on Charter School Finance and Governance, 2009).
5. KIPP, "About KIPP," http://www.kipp.org/about-kipp.
6. Council of Great City Schools, "Fact Sheet and Statistics," http://www.cgcs.org/ domain/24.
7. Ibid.
8. Joe L. Kincheloe, "Why a Book on Urban Education?" in *19 Urban Questions: Teaching in the City,* ed. Shirley R. Steinberg (New York: Peter Lang, 2010), 1–28.
9. Michael Fullan, *The New Meaning of Educational Change* (New York: Teachers College Press, 2007); Ben Levin, *How to Change 5,000 Schools: A Practical and Positive Approach for Leading Change at Every Level* (Cambridge, MA: Harvard Education Press, 2008).
10. Matthew Steinberg, "Does Greater Autonomy Improve School Performance? Evidence from a Regression Discontinuity Analysis in Chicago," *Education Finance and Policy* 9, no. 1 (2014): 1–35; Peggy E. Johnson and Janet H. Chrispeels, "Linking the Central Office and Its Schools for Reform," *Educational Administration Quarterly* 46, no. 5 (2010): 738–775; Lea Hubbard, Hugh Mehan, and Mary Kay Stein, *Reform as Learning: When School Reform Collides with School Culture and Community Politics* (New York: Routledge, 2006).
11. Johnson and Chrispeels, "Linking the Central Office and Its Schools for Reform," 739.
12. Steinberg, "Does Greater Autonomy Improve School Performance?" 3.
13. Janet H. Chrispeels et al., "Aligning Mental Models of District and School Leadership Teams for Reform," *Education and Urban Society* 40, no. 6 (2008): 730.
14. Meredith I. Honig, "District Central Office Leadership as Teaching: How Central Office Administrators Support Principals' Development as Instructional

Leaders," *Educational Administration Quarterly* 48, no. 4 (2012): 733–774.

15. Meredith I. Honig and Thomas Hatch, "Crafting Coherence: How Schools Strategically Manage Multiple, External Demands," *Educational Researcher* 33, no. 16 (2004): 16.

16. Charles L. Thompson, Gary Sykes, and Linda Skrla, *Coherent, Instructionally Focused District Leadership: Toward a Theoretical Account* (East Lansing, MI: Education Policy Center, Michigan State University, 2008), 26.

17. Jonathan A. Supovitz, *The Case for District-Based Reform: Leading, Building, and Sustaining School Improvement* (Cambridge, MA: Harvard Education Press, 2006).

18. Ibid., 3.

19. Ibid., 222

20. Ibid., 223

21. William G. Ouchi, "Power to the Principals: Decentralization in Three Large School Districts," *Organizational Science* 17, no. 2 (2006): 298–307.

22. Ibid., 306

23. Steinberg, "Does Greater Autonomy Improve School Performance?"

24. Stacy M. Childress et al., *Leading for Equity* (Cambridge, MA: Harvard Education Press 2009); Linda Darling-Hammond et al., *Instructional Leadership for Systemic Change: The Story of San Diego's Reform* (Lanham, MD: Scarecrow Education, 2005).

25. Atila Abdulkadiroglu et al., "Accountability and Flexibility in Public Schools: Evidence from Boston's Charters and Pilots," *Quarterly Journal of Economics* 162, no. 2 (2011): 699–748.

26. Thomas J. Peters and Robert H. Waterman, *In Search of Excellence: Lessons from America's Best-Run Companies* (New York: Harper & Row, 1982).

27. Michael L. Tushman and Charles A. O' Reilly, *Winning Through Innovation* (Boston: HBS Press, 2002).

28. David K. Cohen and Deborah Loewenberg Ball, *Instruction, Capacity, and Improvement* (Philadelphia: Consortium for Policy Research in Education, 1999).

29. Ouchi, "Power to the Principals"; Jesper Schmidt Hansen and Marguerite Roza, *Decentralized Decisionmaking for Schools* (Santa Monica, CA: Rand Education, 2005).

30. Center for Collaborative Education, *How Boston Pilot Schools Use Freedom over Budget, Staffing, and Scheduling to Meet Student Needs* (Boston: Center for Collaborative Education, 2005); *The Essential Guide to Boston Pilot Schools* (Boston: Center for Collaborative Education, 2006); Hansen and Roza, *Decentralized Decisionmaking for Schools.*

CHAPTER 1

1. Associated Press, "Schools Seek End to Desegregation Order," *Victoria Advocate,* September 22, 2002.

2. Ibid.

3. Under NCLB, every state was required to establish a statewide definition of AYP that included annual targets for academic achievement, participation in assessments, graduation rates for high schools, and at least one other academic indicator for elementary and middle schools.

4. Maryland uses an estimated cohort rate that is calculated by dividing the number of high school graduates by the sum of the dropouts for grades 9–12, respectively, in consecutive years, plus the number of high school graduates.

5. Maryland Historical Society, "Baltimore City Teachers Association Records, 1849–2001," http://www.mdhs.org/findingaid/baltimore-city-teachers-association-records-1849-2001-ms-3060.

6. Baltimore City Schools, "Joint Governing Panel Frequently Used Terms," http://www.baltimorecityschools.org/cms/lib/MD01001351/Centricity/Domain/5170/Joint%20Governing%20Panel%20Frequently%20Used%20Terms.pdf.

7. U.S. Census Bureau, "Census 2010 Total Population," http://factfinder2.census.gov/faces/nav/jsf/pages/community_facts.xhtml; U.S. Census Bureau, "Annual Estimates of the Population of Metropolitan and Micropolitan Statistical Areas: April 1, 2010 to July 1, 2011," http://www.census.gov/popest/data/historical/2010s/vintage_2011/metro.html.

8. Rick Martinez, "Riding Herd on Charlotte Schools," *News and Observer*, August 9, 2006.

9. "$8 Million Regional Split Planned in NC's Largest School District," *Associated Press*, February 15, 2007.

10. Charlotte-Mecklenburg Schools, "Zones," http://www.cms.k12.nc.us/Learning Zones/Pages/default.aspx.

11. Ibid.

12. Ann Doss Helms, "Charlotte Schools under Fire," *Charlotte Observer*, October 20, 2010.

13. Ibid.

14. Dedrick Russell, "CMS Teachers Outraged about Plan to Tamper with Their Salary," WBTV, http://www.wbtv.com/story/14362672/cms-teachers-outraged-about-plan-to-tamper-with-their-salary?redirected=true.

15. Helms, "Charlotte Schools under Fire,"

16. Stacey Childress et al., *Leading for Equity* (Cambridge, MA: Harvard Education Press, 2009); Stacey Childress and Andrew Goldin, *The Turnaround at Highland Elementary School* (Boston: Harvard Business Press and Harvard University Public Education Leadership Project, 2009); Karen Mapp et al., *Race, Accountability, and the Achievement Gap(A)* (Boston: Harvard Business Press and Harvard University Public Education Leadership Project, 2006); Geoff Marietta, *The Unions in Montgomery County Public Schools* (Cambridge, MA: Harvard Education Press, 2011).

17. The Baldrige Program is a public-private partnership formed to improve

performance of organizations in the United States. It provides organizational assessment tools and criteria and gives out the Malcolm Baldrige National Quality Award.

18. Lucinda Gray, Amy Bitterman, and Rebecca Goldring, *Characteristics of Public School Districts in the United States: Results from the 2011–12 Schools and Staffing Survey* (Washington, DC: National Center for Education Statistics, 2013).

CHAPTER 2

1. Frederick W. Taylor, *The Principles of Scientific Management* (New York: Harper & Brothers, 1911); David B. Tyack, *The One Best System: A History of American Urban Education,* (Cambridge, MA: Harvard University Press, 1974).

2. Ellwood P. Cubberley, *Public School Administration* (Boston: Houston-Mifflin, 1916), 337.

3. Tyack, *The One Best System,* 28.

4. Priscilla Wohlstetter and Susan Albers Mohrman, *School-Based Management: Organizing for High Performance* (San Francisco: Jossey-Bass, 1994); William G. Ouchi, "Power to the Principals: Decentralization in Three Large School Districts," *Organizational Science* 17, no. 2 (2006): 298–307

5. Jerome T. Murphy, "The Paradox of Decentralizing Schools: Lessons from Business, Government, and the Catholic Church," *Phi Delta Kappan* 70, no. 10 (1989): 808–812

6. Rebecca Lish, "Montgomery County's Seven Keys Lead to College Readiness," *American Association of School Administrators,* http://www.aasa.org/content .aspx?id=11940.

CHAPTER 3

1. Amy Edmondson "Psychological Safety and Learning Behavior in Work Teams," *Administrative Science Quarterly* 44, no. 2 (1999): 350–383.

2. Mona Mourshed et al., *How the World's Most Improved School Systems Keep Getting Better* (New York: McKinsey, 2010).

3. Meredith I. Honig, "District Central Office Leadership as Teaching: How Central Office Administrators Support Principals' Development as Instructional Leaders," *Educational Administration Quarterly* 48, no. 4 (2012): 733–774; Meredith I. Honig and Thomas Hatch, "Crafting Coherence: How Schools Strategically Manage Multiple, External Demands," *Educational Researcher* 33, no. 16 (2004): 16–30; Meredith I. Honing, "District Central Offices as Learning Organizations: How Sociocultural and Organizational Learning Theories Elaborate District Central Office Administrators Participation in Teaching and Learning Improvement Efforts." *American Journal of Education* 114, no. 4 (2008): 627–664; Meredith I. Honing et al., *Central Office Transformation for District-Wide Teaching and Learning Improvement* (Seattle: Center for the Study of Teaching

and Policy, University of Washington, 2010); Meredith I. Honing and Lydia R. Rainey, "Autonomy and School Improvement: What Do We Know and Where Do We Go from Here?" *Educational Policy* 26, no. 3 (2012): 465–495. Meredith I. Honig, "District Central Office Leadership as Teaching: How Central Office Administrators Support Principals' Development as Instructional Leaders," *Educational Administration Quarterly* 48, no. 4 (2012): 733–774.

CHAPTER 4

1. Michael Lipsky, *Street-Level Bureaucracy: Dilemmas of the Individual in Public Service* (New York: Russell Sage Foundation, 2010).
2. Haberman Educational Foundation, "The Star Teacher Pre-Screener," http://www.habermanfoundation.org/starteacherprescreener.aspx.

CHAPTER 5

1. Edgar H. Schein, *Organizational Culture and Leadership* (San Francisco: Jossey-Bass, 2010).
2. Ibid.
3. Thomas J. Peters and Robert H. Waterman, *In Search of Excellence: Lessons from America's Best-Run Companies* (New York: Harper & Row, 1982).
4. Richard T. Pascale and Anthony G. Athos, *The Art of Japanese Management: Applications for American Executives* (New York: Simon & Schuster, 1981).
5. James Heskett, *The Culture Cycle: How to Shape the Unseen Force That Transforms Performance* (Upper Saddle River, NJ: FT Press, 2012).
6. Amy C. Edmondson, *Teaming: How Organizations Learn, Innovate, and Compete in the Knowledge Economy* (Boston: Harvard Business Press, 2012); Jody H. Gittell, *The Southwest Airlines Way* (New York: McGraw-Hill, 2003).
7. Pasi Sahlberg, "Lessons from Finland," *American Educator* 35, no. 2 (2011): 32–36; Monica Higgins et al., "Examining Organizational Learning in Schools: The Role of Psychological Safety, Experimentation, and Leadership that Reinforces Learning," *Journal of Educational Change* 13, no. 1 (2012): 67–94.
8. For example, achievement gaps between different racial and ethnic groups across all grade levels declined by double digits from 2003 to 2010. Now, 86 percent of Montgomery County students go to college, including nearly 80 percent of African American students and more than 75 percent of Latino students. Nearly 50 percent of all former Montgomery County students earn a college degree within six years of graduation—a rate nearly double that of the nation as a whole. See Maryland State Department of Education, "2010 Maryland Report Card—Assessments: Montgomery County," http://mdreportcard.org/Assessments.aspx.
9. Amy C. Edmondson, *Teaming: How Organizations Learn, Innovate, and Compete in the Knowledge Economy* (Boston: Harvard Business Press, 2012).

10. Heskett, *The Culture Cycle.*

CHAPTER 6

1. Aldine Independent School District. "Annual Performance Report 2006–2007," www.aldine.k12.tx.us%2Fsections%2Fabout%2Faccountability%2F0607_APR %2Fdistrict.pdf.
2. Aldine Independent School District. "Annual Performance Report 2010–2011," www.aldine.k12.tx.us%2Fsections%2Fabout%2Faccountability%2F1011_APR %2Fdistrict.pdf.
3. Allen Grossman et al., *Meeting New Challenges at Aldine Independent School District (B)* (Cambridge, MA: Harvard Business Press and Harvard University Public Education Leadership Project, 2011).
4. Ibid.
5. Charlotte-Mecklenburg Schools, "2011–2012 Community Guide to Understanding the CMS Budget," http://www.cms.k12.nc.us/News/Pages/CMSbudet presentation.aspx.
6. Michael Winerip, "Helping Teachers Help Themselves," *New York Times*, June 5, 2011, http://www.nytimes.com/2011/06/06/education/06oneducation.html.
7. Texas Education Agency, "Historical Overview of Testing in Texas," www.tea.state .tx.us%2FWorkArea%2FDownloadAsset.aspx%3Fid%3D2147494058&ei=lJwI VJiuIcmxyATh6oHoCA&usg=AFQjCNGhw-gvEsGOU3TPsZsgAryWFd_Xgw &bvm=bv.74649129,d.aWw.
8. Christine Stutz, "The Education of Andrés Alonso," *Baltimore Magazine*, March 2008, http://www.baltimoremagazine.net/old-site/people/2008/03/the-education-of-andr-s-alonso.
9. Ibid.
10. Aldine Independent School District, "School Board Members," http://www .aldine.k12.tx.us/sections/about/leadership/schoolBoard/members.cfm.
11. Grossman et al., *Baltimore City Public Schools.*
12. Ibid.
13. Dropout rates declined from 9.4 percent in 2006 to 4.2 percent in 2010. Graduation rates were at 71.9 percent in 2011. Graduation rates are calculated using the Lever Rate. Maryland Department of Education, "2011 Maryland Report Card: Baltimore City Schools," http://www.mdreportcard.org. Erica L. Green, "City Schools Special Education Legal Fight Ends," *Baltimore Sun*, September 20, 2012.
14. Thomas G. Carroll et al., *Fifty Years after* Brown v. Board of Education*: A Two-Tiered Education System* (Washington, DC: National Commission on Teaching and America's Future, 2014).
15. R. Kenneth Godwin et al., "Sinking Swann: Public School Choice and the Resegregation of Charlotte's Public Schools," *Review of Policy Research* 23, no. 5 (2006): 983–997.

16. Nina H. Clarke and Lillian B. Brown, *History of the Black Public Schools of Montgomery County, Maryland 1872–1961* (Austin, TX: Bartleby Press, 1995).

17. Karen Mapp et al., *Race, Accountability, and the Achievement Gap (A)* (Boston: Harvard Business Press and Harvard University Public Education Leadership Project, 2006); Karen Mapp et al., *Race, Accountability, and the Achievement Gap (B)* (Boston: Harvard Business Press and Harvard University Public Education Leadership Project, 2006).

18. Mapp et al., *Race, Accountability, and the Achievement Gap (A)*; Mapp et al., *Race, Accountability, and the Achievement Gap (B)*.

19. Ben Franklin, "Minority Parents Fight Maryland School Panel," *New York Times*, March 1, 1982.

20. Susan Ferrechio, "Schools Appeal for Return of Race-Based Admissions," *Washington Times*, November 3, 1999.

21. *Annual Report on the System-Wide Outcome Measures, Success for Every Student Plan* (Rockville, MD: Montgomery County Public Schools, 1998).

22. Mapp et al., *Race, Accountability, and the Achievement Gap (A)*.

CONCLUSION

1. Karl E. Weick, "Educational Organizations as Loosely Coupled Systems," *Administrative Science Quarterly* 21, no. 1 (1976): 1–19; Karl E. Weick, "Administering Education in Loosely Coupled Schools," *Phi Delta Kappan*, 63, no. 10 (1982): 673–676.

2. Paul Berman and Milbrey Wallin McLaughlin, *An Exploratory Study of School District Adaptation* (Santa Monica, CA: RAND, 1979).

APPENDIX

1. Jerome T. Murphy, "The Paradox of Decentralizing Schools: Lessons from Business, Government, and the Catholic Church," *Phi Delta Kappan* 70, no. 10 (1989): 808–812; *How Boston Pilot Schools Use Freedom over Budget, Staffing, and Scheduling to Meet Student Needs* (Boston: Center for Collaborative Education, 2005); *The Essential Guide to Boston Pilot Schools* (Boston: Center for Collaborative Education, 2006).

ACKNOWLEDGMENTS

No useful book about the relationship between the central office and schools is written without the willing participation of the champions in the field. We are incredibly grateful to the superintendents—Andrés Alonso, Wanda Bamberg, Peter Gorman, Josh Starr, and Chris Steinhauser—for opening their districts' doors to our inquiry. We are also indebted to the many central office leaders and principals who candidly discussed the successes and challenges they experienced working in large, urban school districts.

This book also exists because of Harvard University's Public Education Leadership Project (PELP), generously funded by the Harvard Business School Class of 1963 and supported by Dean Nitin Nohria at Harvard Business School and Dean James E. Ryan at the Harvard Graduate School of Education. We deeply appreciate their commitment to collaboration and improving leadership in public education.

We also want to give special recognition and thanks to John Kim, faculty member at Harvard Business School and current cochair of PELP. John arrived after we had launched the study and eagerly jumped in, accompanying us on site visits, writing analytical memos, and discussing our findings at length. He made important contributions as we defined and shaped the ideas for this book. We are also indebted to past PELP faculty members, especially Stacey Childress and Richard Elmore, who helped develop the PELP Coherence Framework, which served as the foundation for our analysis of our data.

We're grateful to others who made critical contributions to data collection and analysis. Beth Faller, James Noonan, Elisha Brookover, and Katherine Casey, research assistants on this project, contributed valuable research skills and perceptive insights. Matt Tallon and Deirdre Duckett, PELP's program coordinators over the years, provided outstanding logistical and planning support. We also appreciate the encouragement and feedback from editor extraordinaire Caroline Chauncey and all the help of the Harvard Ed Press staff.

Finally, thanks to all the practitioners and scholars who are still hard at work trying to figure out how to make school districts work better.

ABOUT THE AUTHORS

Susan Moore Johnson is the Jerome T. Murphy Research Professor in Education at the Harvard Graduate School of Education, where she served as academic dean from 1993 to 1999. A former high school teacher and administrator, Johnson has a continuing research interest in the work of teachers and the reform of schools. She has studied the leadership of superintendents, the effects of collective bargaining on schools, priorities of local union leaders, teacher evaluation, use of incentive pay plans for teachers, and school as a context for adult work. Since 1998 she has directed the multiyear research study The Project on the Next Generation of Teachers, which examines how best to recruit, support, and retain a strong teaching force. Johnson has published five books and many articles about these topics. She is a member of the National Academy of Education.

Geoff Marietta is an instructor in education and a doctoral candidate at the Harvard Graduate School of Education. He has worked as a research associate with the Public Education Leadership Project since earning his master's in business administration from Harvard Business School in 2007. Before Harvard, Marietta taught high school special education and was an assistant principal in the Navajo Nation in New Mexico. He has written policy reports on labor-management collaboration, early childhood education, and district leadership for foundations and research institutions and coauthored dozens of Harvard case studies. His research focuses on how social interactions and managerial decisions influence collaboration and learning.

Monica C. Higgins joined the Harvard faculty in 1995 and is the Kathleen McCartney Professor of Education Leadership at the Graduate School of Education (HGSE), where her research and teaching focus on the areas of leadership development and organizational change. Prior to joining HGSE, she spent eleven years as a member of the faculty at Harvard Business School in the Organizational Behavior Unit. Higgins's teaching has focused on the areas of leadership and organizational behavior, teams, entrepreneurship, and strategic human resources management. She is studying the effectiveness of senior leadership teams in large urban school districts across the United States and the conditions that enhance organizational learning in public school systems. In addition, she has a study under way that examines entrepreneurship in education. Higgins currently holds an appointment as a consultant to the U.S. Secretary of Education.

Karen L. Mapp is a senior lecturer on education at the Harvard Graduate School of Education (HGSE) and the faculty director of the Education Policy and Management master's program. Over the past twenty years, her research and practice focus has been on the cultivation of partnerships among families, community members, and educators that support student achievement and school improvement. She has served as the co-coordinator with Mark Warren of the Community Organizing and School Reform Research Project and as a core faculty member in the Doctorate in Educational Leadership Program at HGSE. Mapps is a founding member of the District Leaders Network on Family and Community Engagement, is a trustee of the Hyams Foundation in Boston, and is on the board of the Institute for Educational Leadership. From 2011 to 2013 she served as a consultant on family engagement to the U.S. Department of Education in the Office of Innovation and Improvement. Prior to joining HGSE in January 2005, she served for eighteen months as the deputy superintendent for family and community engagement for the Boston Public Schools.

Allen Grossman was appointed a Harvard Business School professor of management practice in July 2000. He joined that faculty in July 1998 with a concurrent appointment as a visiting scholar at the Harvard Graduate School of Education. Grossman served as president and chief executive officer of Outward Bound USA for six years before stepping down in 1997 to work on the challenges of creating high-performing, mission-focused organizations. He has authored or coauthored three books, forty case studies, and numerous articles. His current research focuses on how to lead and govern high-performing nonprofit organizations and on building effective leadership and management for urban public school districts.

INDEX